Things I Should Have Said To My Father

Things I Should Have Said To My Father

POIGNANT, FUNNY AND UNFORGETTABLE REMEMBRANCES FROM MEMORABLE SONS

❧ compiled by **Joanna Powell** ❧

AVON BOOKS ◭ NEW YORK

THINGS I SHOULD HAVE SAID TO MY FATHER is an original publication of Avon Books. This work has never before appeared in book form.

Permissions by contributors are listed on pages 115–125 of this book.

AVON BOOKS
A division of
The Hearst Corporation
1350 Avenue of the Americas
New York, New York 10019

Copyright © 1994 by Joanna Powell
Published by arrangement with the compiler
Library of Congress Catalog Card Number: 93-39480
ISBN: 0-380-77348-1

Powell, Joanna.
    Things I should have said to my father / Joanna Powell.
    p. cm.
    1. Fathers and sons.   2. Interpersonal relations.   I. Title.
HQ756.P69 1994   93-39480
306.874'2—dc20   CIP

First Avon Books Trade Printing: May 1994

AVON TRADEMARK REG. U.S PAT. OFF. AND IN OTHER COUNTRIES, MARCA REGISTRADA, HECHO EN U.S.A.

Printed in the U.S.A.

OPM   10   9   8   7   6   5   4   3   2   1

I saw a hat in a Salvation Army store,
Just like the one my father wore;
I tried it on, and cracked the brim—
Still trying to be just like him . . .
                              —Chet Atkins

Contents

Preface:
The Struggle for
Lost Words

Convincing a man to talk about his father can be like poking a splinter with a scalding needle. "What a good idea," he says, then leaves skid marks as he runs the other way. The pain that lurks in the shadowy back porches of family memories can trigger the most undignified behavior. As the queen of the four-hankie interview, Barbara Walters, once observed, "The time guests become the most emotional, when the walls really come tumbling down, is when they talk of their fathers."

The premise of this book is simple: Why do two men who love each other have such a hard time saying so? The answers are not so easy. When I posed the question to scores of prominent men I was surprised at the difficulty they had articulating their responses. They seemed to grieve unexpressed love, yet had trouble defining what they wished they had said. Evidence mounted that even the best paternal relationships have raw corners.

Much time was spent nagging, hounding, trading phone calls, pleading by fax. Excuses piled up. Many I approached said they didn't have time to do the project justice. The Broadway actor, Frankie Faison, was candid when summing up two months of phone hide-and-seek. "I think one of the reasons we've been missing each other," he said, "is that I really haven't had time to sit down and deal with my father's death. I know I've been putting our interview off."

Fortunately, there were plenty of courageous souls who felt they had been wrong to settle for a little Indian wrestling, some sports chat, or a distant nod and smile at the end of a meal.

Some, like CNN talk show host Larry King and Fred Rogers

of "Mister Rogers" fame, are so devoted to their father's memory that love and anecdotes spewed forth with little prompting.

Most everyone longed to thank their fathers for the legacies and lessons handed down. Many expressed curiosity about his personal happiness. Was he fulfilled by his life? How deep were the disappointments? When did he give up his dreams? How did he get bitter and beaten down?

In almost all cases, there was regret. Conflict is an inevitable umbilical cord joining boyhood and paternity. Sons remember the silence, the distance, the rage and irritability. And sadly, in many cases, they recall a father's absence.

What's reassuring about the cool remove that shades a son's love is the ultimate forgiveness he is willing to offer.

This book is a collection of personal reflections, from interviews and previously published sources, which each in its own way examines the unspoken words lost between the generations. I hope the vivid, heartfelt honesty of these voices will serve as a catalyst for anyone who has ever hung up the phone with his father leaving important thoughts unsaid.

Everybody who writes a book feels an outpouring of gratitude to those who have stood by them when they behaved like subhumans. I want to thank Jeanne Stahlman, Martha Babcock, and Greg Sandow for their smart and selfless help, my editor Bob Mecoy for conceiving this project, Kris Dahl for her infallible agenting, Michelle Green for her enduring powers as job fairy, my mother for her dogged encouragement, and my five-year-old daughter, Eva, for amusing herself while I "typed."

To my own father, with whom I rarely talk, there are things I should have said: I can't pretend you weren't strict, sometimes harshly so. But I cherish my memories of your playful side, and I'll always smile at the stories you'd tell when I woke up scared in the night. I especially liked the tales of near disaster—when you almost drowned in basic training and when you fainted during medical school. I loved playing "pillow-head" and still feel sad that those games stopped. Now that I'm a grown-up, I can see the gentleness behind your stern demeanor. It comforts me to no longer be frightened of you. I love you.

—Joanna Powell
New York City,
January 1994

Things I Should Have Said To My Father

I

GRATITUDE

Legacies

When I went to Yale Drama School my father, who was a carpenter, came up to visit. The buildings there are fantastic. They're beautiful. I took him into a courtyard and he couldn't believe the stonework. He crawled behind the bushes of a building where people were living. They were looking out the window and were sort of startled to see my father kneeling there, running his hands over the stone.

I explained to him how a lot of immigrants from Italy built most of the campus in the 1700s and 1800s, and that the second part was built during the Depression.

"They used to take them off the boat, put them to work, and then bury them," I said rather cynically.

My father, still admiring the stone, looked at me and said, "Who cares? Look what they built!"

He couldn't get over it. Even though these men had been taken advantage of, they still did something that outlasted their lives.

That spirit of his lives on in me: It's about giving something away, contributing, rather than just taking. It's something a lot of people from that world did, regardless of the obstacles against them.

—John Turturro *(actor)*

*

Over the years I've gotten to feel closer and closer to him. I remember his voice and his laugh. He passed on to me my humor and my addiction to sports and my passion for what I do. I love what I do. I love getting up in the morning. I like smelling the world. I remember him walking with me in the park at night and that smell. He had a great exuberance and a get-up-off-the-floor attitude. But I'm

3

most like him in sense of humor. He liked holding people mesmerized. I do too.

—LARRY KING *(radio and television talk show host)*

*

They say the apple never falls far from the tree. It's true in my case. I learned from my father how to belch and many other useful qualities in life. Eventually, however, the tree falls down. When this happens all that's left is usually a rotten apple lying on the ground and nobody's very happy about it. Especially the apple. But it's a fairly humorless, constipated nerd who blames his father for his troubles, even if his father caused most of them, which is extremely unlikely.

My father and I have always gotten along pretty well, which is probably mostly because I have such a high level of self-absorption that I never noticed we weren't getting along. Fortunately, my father didn't either. Somehow, in spite of the popular notion that the father never had time for the son or the son never appreciated the father until it was too late, my father and I have managed to maintain a warm relationship. Tedious at times, but warm.

He taught me never to eat pasta wearing a white shirt, always to treat adults like children and children like adults, and always to keep the shower curtain inside the tub.

He also taught me to be my own man and not go through life blaming others for my own failures. Fortunately, my high level of self-absorption has come in handy once again. For I'm not afraid of failure and I'm not afraid of success. I'm not afraid to live and I'm not afraid to die. I'm not afraid to fall in love and I'm not afraid to live alone. I'm just afraid that I may have to stop talking about myself for five minutes.

My dad says that would be fine.

—KINKY FRIEDMAN *(singer, songwriter, mystery author)*

I went to the funeral home before anyone else. I had to go there with a comb and hair spray and, you know, fix him up. This weird stuff came over me. I started screaming, "I love you! I want you to know that!" It was too much, his dying then. I wanted to buy him a ranch, to put him back to his roots. He never knew that was my intention. . . . I decided to make my father proud of me till the day I die. Since his death I don't take s—— from anybody. I don't care if it's a studio head, director or producer. If you try to make me sacrifice my standards, if you cross that line with me, I'll go into my Texas macho. I'll hurt you.

—PATRICK SWAYZE *(actor)*

🍃

Strangely enough I found myself with a strong interest in spirituality. I was raised by my mother who was Jewish. But I was very interested in Christianity and Hinduism and Buddhism and for a long time I thought this was just an interest of mine.

Then one day about six years ago I was talking to my father's first wife, whom I've maintained a friendship with all these years, and I told her a little about what I was into: That I had started doing meditation and yoga and that I was really happy. That it had changed my life to some extent and that I thought it was making me a better human being. I had found my teacher, my guru, those kinds of things. I didn't want to say too much because I thought, this is a Texas girl who probably doesn't know too much about this, let alone have an interest.

She nearly floored me when she said, "Oh that's interesting. Your father used to do all of that too."

"You're kidding!" I said.

When he was young and she was dating him in Pampa, Texas, he used to take courses and study meditation and read books on Eastern philosophy. She described some of the things he did, and I instantly recognized that we had shared something much deeper than I had ever imagined. I went home and started going through some of his things, some of his books that ended up with me. Sure enough, I found books on Eastern philosophy, yoga, meditation, books about work on one's personal self that he had studied. He had written into the margins—he was a great underliner and big note taker—and I found that it was so wonderful to share his thoughts some fifty years later.

Because it wasn't of interest to his friends and companions, none of them ever told me anything about it.

—ARLO GUTHRIE *(folk singer,*
son of seminal American
songwriter WOODY GUTHRIE*)*

My father had an extraordinary affection for me. He was the silliest man I ever knew and yet cruelly shrewd. He thought and talked of me up to his last breath. I was very fond of him always, being a sinner myself, and even liked his faults. Hundreds of pages and scores of characters in my books came from him. His dry (or rather wet) wit and his expression of face convulsed me often with laughter . . . I got from him his portraits, a waistcoat, a good tenor voice, and an extravagant licentious disposition (out of which, however, the greater part of any talent I may have springs).

—JAMES JOYCE, 1882–1941
(Irish poet and author)

My father was very dashing—I'd see him in a tuxedo, with his silver flute, and girls singing around him. He'd take me at 5:00 p.m. to Studio 8H at NBC, and put me in the glass box so I could watch Toscanini, and there'd be a knob in there that controlled the volume, and that just blew me away when I was a kid, when I realized that picture and sound were not connected! There was a tremendous amount of magical, emotional, mystical stuff connected to family. . . . That part of life is very attractive to me.

—FRANCIS FORD COPPOLA
(film director)

My dad used to take me to his office on Saturdays when I was a boy and he'd let me use the adding machine and typewriter and intercom phone. I loved those times, so I often think of him when I'm in my own office or in a store that sells office supplies. One of the things Dad liked most of all was to grow pine trees. I'll always remember our last conversation—just a few days before he died (in 1970). The last thing he told me was the nursery he felt was the best place to buy seedlings. He loved growing things, and whenever I see a particularly splendid blue spruce (one of his special favorites) I invariably think of Dad. A friend of ours gave me a spruce seedling for Christmas. I'm looking forward to planting it with my grandson (Alexander) in his back yard.

Dad was a "secret giver." I remember so vividly walking with him on the sidewalks of New York. He would place dimes on windowsills. When I asked him about that he said, "I just like to think about how glad people will be to find them." Obviously he made many people glad in many ways during his wonder-filled life. I'm blessed to have been able to be his son.

There is always unfinished business in any significant life relationship; but, just as it is with pine trees, human beings have the chance to grow both here and beyond. Dad and I have things to teach [to] and learn from each other in eternity. That should be just about enough time.

—FRED ROGERS
(TV host of
"Mr. Rogers' Neighborhood")

To this day, my father is almost a mythical figure to me. Throughout my life, I've picked up bits and pieces about what a colorful character he was long before I was born. But I'm sure I'll never know all of it. He told the stories and I listened, but I never asked for them. I was just grateful when the stories came along. In my growing up years, I always had the sense that I could live to be two hundred and never lead a life quite as interesting as my dad's. Maybe it happens that way a lot. Maybe you're lucky if you've got a father who always seemed tougher and quicker on his feet than you could ever be. Or would have to be.

—REGGIE JACKSON
(former pro baseball player)

❦

There are always things you'd like to say that go better left unsaid. The hard part is to find the right time to express a belief or an emotion or a fear. And with our family, five distinctly different children, there are things that will probably never be said and are probably better not said.

My dad wasn't around much when we were kids because he was working or sailing. I'd sometimes think, geez why is he gone so much. But now as I get older I realize that there's such a thing as work. That I need to make a living. I can do the nine-to-five stint. But it takes more to be successful.

Now I'm back working for Turner and putting in as many hours a day as I can and stay sane. I don't have a wife and children now. But if I did, they would be hurt by that. And if I were also sailing at the same time, that would take up most of my time.

His priorities may not have been a hundred percent correct. But would I take it back? Well, dad would have been home more if he hadn't worked as hard. Then he wouldn't have been as successful, and therefore I wouldn't be where I am today. In retrospect, he did exactly the right thing. At the time, I didn't think it was right.

I'm glad he's done what he's done. I haven't told him that though. The other kids are coming of age now, entering their adult lives, and some of them are still a little angry. I try to sit down with them and get them to look at the choices—the pluses and the minuses of our family. The pluses far outweigh the minuses.

So I say, Yes Dad, you were a great father, but in a different way than great fathers are in the normal way of looking at things. But what about Ted Turner is normal?

—TED TURNER IV
(son of media mogul TED TURNER*)*

I'm grateful to my father [Louis Ginsberg] for poetry love—of Poe, Whitman, Shelley, Keats, Milton, Shakespeare, E. A. Robinson. He gave me tenderness toward sentient existence and its expression in cadenced poetry. . . . Would that all sons' fathers were poets! For the poem and the world are the same.

—ALLEN GINSBERG *(Beat poet)*

We lived in Myra, on the upper Mud River, which was just a few farmhouses, a post office, and a country store. Our white clapboard house stood next to a cornfield. When I was about three, we moved to Hubble, where Dad went to work for the railroad. I remember him coming home with his face and hands bandaged from a flash fire when he shoveled coal into the firebox. As young as I was, that incident made a deep impression: I realized for the first time how hard he struggled to shelter us from the cold. Until then, I had no idea what Dad was up against, how tough life really was. But Dad wasn't a brooder or complainer. In fact, he was a great prankster, and a real marksman with a slingshot. An old lady neighbor had a milking cow and every evening she'd come out and milk it in a field next to the railroad tracks. Dad would sit on the porch and shoot pebbles at that cow; the old lady milking on the other side couldn't figure out why Bessie kept kicking over her bucket . . .

Although Mom raised us, I think I was more "turned" like Dad, which is West Virginia for "taking after." I'm stubborn and strong-willed too, and opinionated as hell. My folks weren't well-educated, but they never lacked country wisdom and common sense. As hard as Dad worked, he enjoyed it, and that was an important lesson, too. Tramping alone through the woods with a rifle, or in a cockpit with a throttle in my hands—that's where I was happiest. And that's how I've lived my life.

My beginnings back in West Virginia tell who I am to this day. My accomplishments as a pilot tell more about luck, happenstance, and a person's destiny. But the guy who broke the sound barrier was the kid who swam

the Mud River with a swiped watermelon, or shot the
head off a squirrel before school.

—CHUCK YEAGER
*(Air Force general and first pilot
to exceed the sound barrier)*

🍃

I'm just amazed when I catch a glimpse of who I really
am. Just a little flash like the gesture of my hand in a
conversation and WHAM, there's my old man. Right
there, living inside me like a worm in the wood. And
I ask myself, "Where have I been all this time?"

—SAM SHEPARD
(playwright and actor)

🍃

I'm grateful for my father's historical and cultural contribution
to society and music. His contribution to African-American
culture. Being an icon in all of those areas was
obviously inspiriting. My dad excelled at a time when
Black men weren't given the opportunity to excel in this
country. That was a tremendous role model for me.

He gave us a work ethic. It was frustrating as a kid
having your father on the road upwards of forty weeks
a year, but by the same token he instilled in us a purpose:
if you have a job to do you've got to go do it. In some
cases you've got to go to the ends of the earth to do
it. I learned a great deal from that. That nobody was
going to give it to you. You had to go work for it.

From my dad's perspective, he didn't want us to be deluded
by the fact that we were an anomaly in 1950's
American culture: wealthy Black people living in a
predominately white environment. He didn't want us to
think that because we had lived a certain life of privilege
that we were privile*ged* or better than anyone else. And
we were reminded that even though we were living in
an Anglo environment, we were not to forget that we were
Black and not to think we were better than anyone else.

He instilled in us that what was his was ours, but
ultimately what was yours was yours. You've got to

work, not just sit on your ass and wait for the old man
to die and inherit a million bucks.

> —ED ECKSTINE
> *(president of Mercury Records,*
> *son of jazz great* BILLY ECKSTINE*)*

My father, Benito Mussolini, was a good musician. It wasn't
his profession, of course. But he played the violin, he could
read well, and he loved symphonic music—Puccini,
Verdi, Wagner. When I was young, he was very proud
that I played the piano. I wish I had lived to come to
one of my concerts.

My father was not against jazz. I played Fats Waller
records in the house, and he never told me to turn them
off.

> —ROMANO MUSSOLINI *(jazz pianist,*
> *son of the Italian fascist dictator)*

My father was the police chief of Riviera Beach, Florida.
The fact that he was the police chief created all sorts
of tensions because my friends would say, "You can't
do this and you can't do that, your father's the police
chief!" So, of course, I had to do everything first.
First to dive off the bridge, first one to punch
someone in the nose, first one to speed. I ran away
from home when I was fourteen. Thank God there
were no drugs back then! I lost all nine lives and two
extra ones.

We have a saying in the South: no man is a man until
his pappy tells him. And mine never did. So—even
though what I wanted most from my father was an enormous
hug—until recently I would have guys come over to box
with me . . .

Parts of it are still going on, even today. My dad was
with me recently on the airstrip on my ranch and I was
showing off again in my car, practically flying the car through
the air. I still want his approval.

> —BURT REYNOLDS *(actor)*

My father was a driver. He liked to get in the car and just drive. He got everybody else in the car too, and he made us drive. He made us all drive.

—BRUCE SPRINGSTEEN
(singer, songwriter)

I guess my favorite memories are of having a father. I have a whole five years of memories. I remember when Alice the cat died and my father was crying; I remember watching TV with him; wrestling and jumping up and down with him in my room; going to Central Park and riding in the horse carriage together. We did a lot of drawing. He would scribble in circles and squiggles on a piece of paper, and I would have to turn it into whatever I saw in them. We took turns doing it to see who could make more things out of the squiggles. That was a game I loved to play. With him, every day was an adventure. It was like my dad and I were buddies, and there was no real sorrow then.

—SEAN LENNON
(son of The Beatles' JOHN LENNON*)*

We had a reception at our house after [the funeral]. I went up to my father's room, and I lay on my father's bed. He had pictures on his wall of my aunt Kick [Kathleen] in her nurse's uniform during the war, and pictures of my Uncle Joe and Jack.

And I remember sitting there thinking they all looked so young and they were all dead. And I lay there and wept for probably an hour or more, and then my father's best friend, Dave Hackett, came in and sat with me. He just sat there silently for I don't know how long, maybe forty minutes or something.

Then he said to me: "He was the best man I ever knew."

. . . My father was a very good father, and I understand that more and more as I raise my own children. He

spent a lot of time with us. He concentrated on our
development. He didn't care so much what area. I was
always interested in wildlife and animals, and he helped
foster that.

We ate dinner together almost every night, which I
now consider incredible, because I know how difficult
that is with my children. He would tell us history stories
at the dinner table. He read us the Bible almost every night.
Our family prayed together. We said the rosary almost
every night. And then we did sports together.

He stressed to us that it was less important to be successful
and prosperous than it was to be people of principles, and
that you don't get happy out of accumulating things.
You get happy out of service.

—ROBERT F. KENNEDY, JR.
(son of ROBERT F. KENNEDY)

When I was about ten, I played little league football and
we always lost. One time my coach didn't show up and
my father coached our team. That was the one game
we almost won. I had always respected my father. But
it was the first time I really understood that he was hip.
Not cool. Hip. He knew what was going on.

He was one of the jazz musicians in the south in the
early 1960s trying to make it. There was still
segregation and not much money. But he was intensely
committed to the art and Afro-American culture. He and
his friends were real men, and the seriousness with
which they approached life affected their surroundings.
They were practicing five and six hours a day. In addition
to being really intense about an art form that nobody really
cared about, he could function in the greater society
and do regular things. After six hours of practice, he
taught his kids how to catch a baseball or win an argument
in the barber shop. He was not pretentious at all, not into
material things like cars or money. And that's
something I've inherited from him that I'm very proud
of. I'm grateful for the way he approached playing jazz,
teaching kids, and the seriousness that he brought to a
conversation. All those things had such joy.

I don't have to tell my father much. He's very intuitive. He knows things about me. When we talk, we mainly have philosophical discussions and I can always ask him for information. But I think I rely on him most to bounce ideas off. He gives me a kind of empowerment that a lot of fathers don't want to give up to their children.

I remember the first time I figured out something about music that I didn't think my father knew. It was about ten years ago, and I was reticent to tell him because I didn't know how he'd take it. When I finally told him, he wasn't intimidated. He was excited. He said, "Tell me again so I can write that down." When you know as much music as my father, it's hard to come up with something new to him. And he found it gratifying, not threatening. Many fathers don't realize they're not giving up their power to their children. Children have their own power. But fathers can give a feeling of power. My father gave me that power.

—WYNTON MARSALIS
(jazz trumpeter, educator,
artistic director of "Jazz
from Lincoln Center") on his
father ELLIS MARSALIS, JR.
(pianist, educator, composer)

Lessons

"**W**hat are you giving up for Lent?" my father said.
"Grapes," I replied.
"Grapes?" asked my father. "We never have grapes."
They were too expensive—if you could get them.
"Well, that's what I'm giving up," I said with an expression
of insufferable martyrdom. After mass that day my father
stopped at the fruit shop in Blackrock and bought a
pound of grapes. My family sat in the car, each one
licking their grapes, peeling them, exclaiming over them,
chewing them, slowly allowing the juice to pour down their
chins. Licking their fingers, they ate them all. They
crammed their cheeks with them, I didn't get one.
"You've given them up," my father gloated.

—SIR BOB GELDOF
(singer, organizer of Live Aid)

*

I can always count on thinking of my father at the same
time each day: when I shave. He recommended a new shaving
cream to me before he died, and he turned out to be right.
We had a chance to get closer before he died. He seemed
pleased with what I'd accomplished in life. My father was
a very reasonable man. Cerebral. A teacher. Sentimental.
Outwardly jovial much of the time, in a way that concealed
a basic Baptist puritanism. Let's just say he wasn't
overconfident. Or materialistic. . . . He was married once.

—WARREN BEATTY *(actor)*

*

"**Y**ou don't have to wave at the waiter like that to get
his attention, lad," Dad told me over dinner at Romanoff's.
"Watch."

He merely twitched his eyebrow, and the waiter
appeared instantly.

Then it was my turn. I spent the rest of the meal trying
to catch the waiter's eye. I'll bet everyone else there
felt sorry Yul's kid suffered from such a terrible twitch.

—ROCK BRYNNER
(son of actor YUL BRYNNER)

🌿

During his last years, Papa needed a full-time nurse, but
even so, he went for strolls, and his favorite pastime was
going to my movies. He saw every one of them at least
six times. I always felt sorry for the nurse.

To Be or Not to Be came to Miami Beach. In the first
scene in the movie I wore a Nazi uniform and was seated
in my office in the theater. Another actor entered and
my right hand shot up in the Nazi salute. "Heil Hitler,"
I said.

My father watched the movie for about one minute and
when he saw this scene he grabbed the nurse's arm
and stomped out of the theater. The nurse couldn't
believe that for once she didn't have to sit through another
Jack Benny picture. I imagine she was the happiest nurse
in all of Florida.

For two weeks I didn't receive the regular weekly
letter. I wrote him. He didn't answer. I telephoned. He was
never "in." Finally, one evening, he answered the phone
instead of the nurse when I called.

"Hello, Dad," I said.

No answer at the other end.

"This is Jack—your son."

"You're no son of mine! I got nothing to discuss with
you."

"What did I do?"

"You gave the salute to Hitler is what you did."

"Did you stay for the whole picture?"

"I should stay for such a picture? I was never so
ashamed in my life. I don't tell people anymore I'm the
father of Jack Benny."

"But that was only the beginning of the picture. If
you had waited you would see that I'm against the

Nazis. I'm fighting them. Please go back and see it all the way through."

So he did. And how he loved that movie now. By his own actual count, Papa saw *To Be or Not to Be* forty-six times.

—JACK BENNY, 1894–1974
(comedian)

🖋

Although my father was a very funny man, he was never truly happy, and I think that he eventually realized his job was a dead end. In spite of this, jobs at Billingsgate were very sought after because of the pay and lack of qualifications needed. You could only get in if you had a relation who already worked there. I remember him saying to me as I grew up that when I went to work, he could get me into the market. He seemed very proud of this, and I had to bite my tongue to stop myself from telling him that I had absolutely no intention of following in his footsteps.

When they eventually began to mechanize Billingsgate, my father gave me the following advice: Never do a job where you can be replaced by a machine. Based on that advice I thought how clever I was to become an actor, little realizing I'd be facing competition from a tin shark, a green frog, and the Terminator. The only other advice that he ever gave me was never to trust anyone who wore a beard, a bow tie, two-tone shoes, sandals, or sunglasses. Having believed him for many years, you can imagine the panic I was in when I arrived in Hollywood.

—MICHAEL CAINE *(actor)*

🖋

I had to go to the county hospital for a tonsillectomy. In a huge room about fifteen children were lined up for an assembly-line operation. I saw one boy lying on the bloody table. I witnessed the whole gory procedure. I started screaming and straining to get away, but my hands and feet were all bound. After they wheeled the boy off, they shoved a mask on me; I felt the suffocating smell of ether. Things started to go round like Fourth of July fireworks, then it became black.

I woke up in a small dormitory with about eight other boys. My father was sitting beside me. He sat there all afternoon.

That night he wouldn't leave when the nurse said the visiting hours were over. He picked me up in his arms and covered me with a blanket. He carried me down the fire escape and all the way home. My mother had said he was rather undemonstrative, but he kissed me that day and took me home.

My mother and my grandmother were terribly upset that he hadn't left me at the hospital. They were afraid that I would have complications, but he said, "No, I'll take care of my son myself." He sat there and he didn't go to work the next day until he was sure that I was all right.

He had to go back and feed the animals [at the zoo where he worked]; the panther had refused to eat. Later, he told me the cat looked around, as if to say, "Where's the little boy? Where's my friend?" And my father started talking to the panther, saying, "He's sick now, but he'll be back in a few days." But she wouldn't eat, just kept pacing and pacing. Finally, he tried to force her to eat; he put his hand inside the cage to hand her the food, and she jumped and practically tore his arm off. He was in the hospital for two weeks hovering between life and death.

I went to see the panther several times while my father was in the hospital. I felt that she was sorry for what she had done. Her deep growl was more like a cry asking me to forgive her. I petted her.

I went to see my father in the hospital and said that I had been to see the cat. I confessed that I had been disloyal to him. He said, "Don't be silly, the cat loves you. And she's right. I had no business fooling around with somebody else's girlfriend. That's what a real woman should be. You should only be lucky enough to find a woman like that in your life, one who will kill anybody else who comes near her. If you ever look for a woman, look for a woman like that cat."

—ANTHONY QUINN *(actor)*

My dad's pretty good at understanding, and I don't take it for granted, because I think a lot of fathers would never be able to understand what their sons go through.

—ETHAN BROWNE
(son of musician JACKSON BROWNE)

It's hard to be a son. You have to somehow get rid of the old man, you gotta get him out of the way. So many people can't accomplish anything until they do. It's also hard to be a parent, because to be a parent you have to grow up. It's hard to put other people first, to be mature. It's easy to put a little baby first. They're the size of a loaf of bread, and they sleep most of the time. But as it goes on they become more and more intelligent and more and more your equal, and of course, eventually, surpass you in so many ways.

—JACKSON BROWNE *(musician)*

My father taught me to play baseball from the time I could walk. He'd take me to the park at the school down the street, and pitch to me, show me how to hit and how to field. He instilled a spark in my brain for winning and never settling for second best. "If you're going to play baseball," he'd say, "do it right."

He was a police officer—a pretty hard-nosed guy. For several years after I was born, he worked two jobs because he was determined to have me living in a house rather than an apartment before I was old enough to know the difference.

Playing baseball with him wasn't a whole lot of fun. It was work. Some people now say that I take this game too seriously. But that's how I learned how to play.

If I ever came up with a personal problem, I don't think I could talk to my father about it. That probably stems from a long time ago when I did have a lot of personal problems that I wanted to talk to him about, and he

was never there. Or he would take the personal problems
I did run into when I was a kid too harshly, or the punishment
would be too deep.

There was a situation when I was dating a girl, when
I was just old enough to date, I had my folks' car. I
was driving and the girl was in the passenger seat, and
I leaned over to give her a kiss, and the car went that way
too. It hit the curb. I corrected myself, not much damage
done, but the hubcap came off. So I put the hubcap
in the back seat, snuck home, and about two o'clock in
the morning I went to the garage to put the hubcap back
on. My dad found out that the hubcap was scratched.
I don't know why I did this, since he's a police officer,
but I told my father that the paramedics were code three
with lights and sirens on, and came up behind me. I had
to pull over to the side and I wasn't watching the curb
because I was looking in the rearview mirror.

My dad threatened me, "Are you sure you're telling me
the truth?" And I said, "Sure I'm telling you the truth."
And he said, "Well, you know I could call up the
paramedics and find out if they were on call that night."
And I thought, Oh, I'm trouble. But he never called. If I
told my dad now, he would probably put his arms around
me and just laugh. But then I was too scared to tell
him, even though no damage was done other than a
scratched hubcap. He would have probably said fix it, no
big deal. But it's funny, why I lied.

—JEFF KENT
(New York Mets second baseman)

🍂

I grew up in the kind of Black family that people today
worry is disappearing. . . . Dad didn't believe in handouts.
So as a kid, the only way I could get my hands on any
spending money was to go out and earn it. By the time
I was ten I had my own little neighborhood business. I
raked leaves, cleaned yards, and shoveled snow. With the
money I earned, I could go to the movies and buy an
occasional record.

Dad was my idol, so I paid close attention to the way

he handled his money. As a way of forcing himself to save, he always kept two or three uncashed checks in his wallet. There were times when I thought he was a little too careful, especially when he wouldn't buy me something I thought I needed. But then I'd hear, "You want five dollars, Junior? Here, take the lawn mower. There's a lot of grass in this town, and I bet you could earn that money real quick."

He hated to borrow, and he often warned us about the dangers of going into debt. One of the happiest days of his life was when he made the final mortgage payment on our house. But he was generous, too. When his friends needed a few bucks, he was always willing to help.

Through basketball and my business interest, I've been blessed with a great income, far more than my father ever dreamed of. A couple of years before Cookie and I got married, I bought a big new house in Beverly Hills that cost me $7.2 million. But I'm still my father's son, and some things just don't change.

When I bought the house, my accountant advised me not to make too large a down payment. For tax purposes, he explained, it was better to pay off the mortgage over many years. I knew he was right, but I just couldn't do it that way. Instead, I put down $6.2 million, which was more than eighty-five percent of the total price. But I still didn't feel right, and a few months later, I wrote out a check for that last million. I just hated the idea of that mortgage—or any debt—hanging over my head.

—Earvin "Magic" Johnson
(former NBA player, L.A. Lakers)

When I was a boy of fourteen, my father was so ignorant I could hardly stand to have the old man around. But when I got to be twenty-one, I was astonished at how much he had learned in seven years.

—*attributed to* Mark Twain,
1835–1910 (American author)

My father was fifty years old when I was born. He was in the streets a lot, a throwback to the old-style man who brings in the money, but doesn't do very much. I've spent more time with my kids now, and the oldest one is fourteen, than he spent with me in a lifetime.

He was an interesting, self-made man who worked as a longshoreman in Newport News, Virginia, loading and unloading ships. He also owned houses which he rented out as boarding houses. He was a gambler, ran numbers, and loved to drink. Still, he always brought the paycheck home.

One time, when I went with him to visit the boarding houses and collect money, he got into a card game called Tonk, which is very popular in Black communities. For the first time, I felt a threat of violence with my father. He carried a gun—everybody did in those circles—and I felt he wouldn't be afraid to use it. He was a big man, about 250 pounds, and he wasn't afraid of anything.

Everybody playing cards had been drinking, and this guy accused him of cheating. He swore up and down that he hadn't—that he'd won. The argument almost exploded into a fight where someone would pull out their gun and shoot the other one. I was really scared. But then the other guy backed down, and my father won all the money.

As we left and were driving home, I challenged him. "Daddy, you cheated, you pulled that card from the bottom," I said. "I saw you."

"Boy, mind your own business," he said. "There are things you just don't understand." That was the end of the conversation.

He knew that I knew he had cheated. But he was giving me a lesson: "If you cheat, make sure you can get away with it. . . . Don't back down." Something like that.

It gave me a strong sense of connection to him and a deeper understanding of him. Everybody in that room was capable of cheating. It didn't make it right. But it happened. And from that day on, he dealt with me on a different level. He realized I had the ability to take things in and that I was just. I was a very religious

young man—trustworthy and righteous. In a weird way,
I got it from him, even though his whole lifestyle was the
complete opposite. I think he really loved seeing that quality
in me.

I wish there had been more times we'd shared. I'd
have liked to have driven across country together. I really
miss him. But he was a man who lived and loved life, and
he passed that on to me.

I guess if there was one thing I could say to him now,
it would be, "Dad, you had a great time in your life, and
I'm not going to stand in judgement of anything you did.
And I'm having a great time in my life, and I know
you wouldn't judge me or anything I do. You let me
live my life."

I'd also tell him, "Pop, don't cheat at cards!"

And he'd say, "Mind your own business, boy, there
are certain things you don't understand!"

—FRANKIE FAISON *(actor)*

*

I think my father would be proud that I did the things
that I thought were important to do. I didn't move to
Hollywood. I really wanted to have a family life with
my wife and my kids in a way that I was not able to
have with him. And I'm not sure I would have been able
to have it with him even if he hadn't been sick, because
of who he was. He decided to be on his own. The fact
that he was sick made that possible. But he would have
found a way to do it anyway.

The truth is I probably would have made that same decision
to leave home and not be there had I not experienced
what it was like for the family. But having lived it from
the family point of view, from a child's point of view, made
me never want to put somebody through that.

I had to juggle between having the same kind of life
as a performer and traveling around and also raising
four kids. So I had to compensate. I took my wife and kids
on the road with me when they were young. I brought
tutors out on the road when they were in school. And
when they started getting into things they had to be
home for—scouts, basketball, or school plays—that's when

I tried to stay home. I'm glad I made that decision, and I think my kids are wonderful.

My father and I might have disagreed over that. But I think he would have respected me as a father.

—ARLO GUTHRIE

I wish he were still around. When I don't know what to do, I often wonder what he'd think and what he would say. . . . [When he was alive] I would say, they want me to do this TV thing, and there's a conflict with this play. I'd freak out because I wouldn't want to turn it down. He would say, "Throughout your life you're going to do that three thousand times. You can't worry about it." He didn't live or die by each job. He seemed to have a very good perspective on that.

—MATTHEW BRODERICK *(actor, son of actor* JAMES BRODERICK*)*

I kept realizing that nobody would be honoring me if Daddy hadn't raised me the way he had. He had never let me get a job, like delivering papers or working at a store. He kept me home out of trouble. I didn't have many advantages, but I had that.

—ARTHUR ASHE, JR., 1943–1993 *(tennis champion)*

Advice that sticks in my mind resulted from a horseback outing we took together at a riding academy. After we started down the riding trial, my father asked me to trade horses with him. I immediately did, and soon after, we came to a large tree that had fallen across the trail. My original horse, with my father now on it, stepped neatly over the log. My horse, meanwhile, took a sudden wild leap, and I sailed over its head into some bramble bushes. My father, laughing, told me "That horse I gave you is a jumper."

"Then why did you give it to me?" I asked crying.

Still grinning, he said, "That'll teach you—never trust your father."

I got used to his humor. You got to be thick-skinned living with him. The thing about him was that he wasn't very thick-skinned himself. If you said something critical, he'd practically faint. But no matter how difficult, he was always funnier than hell. That was a compensating fact.

—ARTHUR MARX
(son of GROUCHO MARX)

He always told me don't lie. You never have to lie. There's no reason ever to lie. It was illogical to him why anyone would have to lie.

I skipped Hebrew school one day and we sat casually down to dinner. He offhandedly asked, "How was Hebrew school today?"

"Fine," I said.

He whacked me. I flew across the room. A friend had told him I wasn't at school that day. And I remember him leaning over me and saying, "Never lie." I don't know anyone who has never lied, but I always had a conscience about it.

—LARRY KING

One day, when we were fishing, Dad said, "Here boy, cast this out for me," and handed me his favorite fishing pole. I went to cast it and the thing just lifted out of my hands and flew into the water. Oh man, I felt so bad about that. He loved that pole. But it was the funniest thing. I said, "Let's go buy a new one. I'll get one, let's go somewhere." I really wanted to replace it. But he said, "No boy, don't worry about it. Forget about it." It was like he knew nobody else would get to use that pole.

—JIMMY SCOTT
(jazz singer, son of ARTHUR SCOTT)

He's my hero. I learned from him never to quit and never to stop striving to improve yourself. He gave me a foundation of belief without which all the fame and success and money would have overwhelmed me.

—MEL GIBSON *(actor)*

He has a wonderful sense of humor, all kinds of self-deprecating humor, and he can be real cute in person—not in a bad way, but in a real charming way, a real guileless kind of way. I've always admired that. He's never tried to come on terribly macho. I hate fathers who are always punching their sons on the shoulder. He's never done that.

On a more gritty note, when I was still living at my parents' house, we were sitting by the pool one day and I was in the flux of some adolescent hormonal surge, and he decided I ought to have a little advice. He told me, "Never sleep with a girl if you're going to be embarrassed to be seen on the street with her the next day."

I think that was more for the girl's benefit than mine. He didn't want me jumping on some girl and then leaving her in the lurch.

—RON REAGAN
(son of former President RONALD REAGAN)

The big memory I have of my father is in the kitchen, cooking. Even though he was a locomotive engineer, he had the cleanest hands of any man I've ever known. His work on the locomotives was with grease, and he'd come home in overalls that were so dirty they would stand by themselves. When I was a small boy, my job was to help him get those dirty overalls off so that they could be washed. Oh, they were dirty. This man worked in grease, and you worked long hours in those days. People keep talking about thirty-five-hour work weeks, thirty-hour work weeks, twenty-seven-hour work weeks. His day

in the busy season was sixteen hours on, eight off.
He ran freight trains, passenger trains, whatever had
to be run. He retired before diesels. God was merciful when
he took my father out of this life while steam was still
the dominant force in railroading. It would have broken
his heart to have seen the end of steam locomotives.
They were his life. After he got his overalls off he would
clean his hands, and then before he began to cook he'd
give them a brush, and when he had them right he
would shake Arm & Hammer baking soda over them
and clean them again. Then he would start to cook.

He was a rugged, physical man in a rugged, physical
man's world, and you would think that he would be
a rough, careless man. But this was what he liked best.
He would get the food ready and he'd put it in the oven,
and then the enjoyment of his day would close in upon
him. He would always have a book—he loved
literature—and he would sit there in the rocking chair
in the kitchen and read. He would roll a cigarette—he didn't
buy tailor-mades, as he called them—and he would sit in
the rocking chair, very gently rocking back and forth,
and read and smoke while the food was slowly cooking.

That was my father at home. He loved and respected
his home, and I caught that from him. He never gave me
any great dissertation about the sanctity of the home
and the joys of the fireside. But I learned it. The
warmest memory I have of this man, this man of clean
hands, was [seeing him] sitting in that rocking chair, rolling
his cigarettes, reading a good book and cooking.

—RED BARBER
(sportscaster and commentator)

When I was a kid and always in combat with my father,
I thought there was something wrong with him, and I was
sane. But you know, I've lied to myself about how I
would be hip when I became a father, how I would have
compassion, how I would be able to handle situations. You
really don't know how tough kids can be—your kids.

—BILL COSBY *(comedian)*

I told him when he was dying that he'd been a role model
of aristocratic pride, arrogance, and independence. And
I thanked him for it. He died in about 1956–57. I'd still
praise him to the sky for it. He gave me an attitude
of independence, an outsider attitude of self-respect
and pride.

Basically I didn't resent that he wasn't there [when I was]
growing up—it taught me to be independent. I feel a
little sorry now that I didn't look him up sooner. But
I have no resentment at all. I think the worst curse is to
have a father who's on your case every second. You do
this with money, you do that, checking on you, smother
love—smother fathers are very crippling.

I never had the idea he was a person judging me. There
was no judgmental stuff about it at all.

—TIMOTHY LEARY
(educator and lecturer)

I'm an only child and my father and I are very close. When
I'm in a bind, I run to him.

One of our conversations led to my song, "Free." I
was on the road and was going through some romantic
problems, so I called him—we talk at least every two days
when I'm touring. I said I was feeling really bad, really
down in the dumps and told him about my relationship
troubles. His advice became the hook of that song: "I'm
free, I'm free, and your problems are only as big as you
want them to be."

He said, as long as you're a good person inside and
live with faith and hope and confidence, your problems
will never really be that big at all. Just remember you are
free. Given that we came to this country from Cuba, it has
special meaning.

—JON SECADA *(recording artist)*

Growing up we were on a shoestring budget. I got my
first car when I was twenty years old. It was a 1976 Plymouth

Voyager van with 160,000 miles on it that somebody
had given to my dad. There wasn't a lot of money
around when we were kids. But when we were old
enough to supposedly know better than to go spend it,
we got trust funds at twenty-five. I promptly went and
spent mine.

I spent it racing sailboats. For three years I got to
race big, offshore sailboats. I tried to put a campaign together
for the Whitbread around-the-world race which is an eight-
million-dollar campaign.

Now there WILL BE NO MORE money. But that was
an opportunity my father gave me. I got to live my
dream.

—TED TURNER IV

I would walk past the saloon at night, its curtains raised
high on the tall windows so that no young boy could peer
over them. I'd hear my father's voice in there, in that
roaring [Yiddish] accent, regaling his drunken cronies
with some story about things that had happened in Russia.
I'd hear them all burst into laughter. It was the world of
men. No women were allowed, and I wasn't allowed
either. I kept waiting for my father to take me by the
hand into the world of men.

Once he gave me just a taste of it, a tease. One hot
summer day, Pa took me by the hand and led me into
a saloon. I can see it so clearly, the streaks of brilliant
sunlight streaming through the window and then the
black shadows in contrast . . . just like the movie sets
that I would later play in. No one was there but the
bartender. My father bought me a glass of loganberry.
Nectar of the gods! I was in the world of men for a brief
moment, even though the men had not yet arrived. But
I was in their habitat. Later on, I would be in those
settings often with Burt Lancaster or John Wayne.
It always made me smile, because it seemed to me that
we were all still children pretending to be in the world
of men.

—KIRK DOUGLAS *(actor)*

One of my earliest memories is of my dad and me walking across the street in front of our house in Colorado. He had whiskey in a glass with ice cubes, and I tasted it. He told me I wouldn't like it, and I didn't.

—Gus Van Sant, Jr.
(film director)

The most important influence on me, growing up, was my father, Fred Trump. I learned a lot from him about toughness in a very tough business. I learned about motivating people, and I learned about competence and efficiency: get it done, get it done right, and get out.

—Donald Trump
(real estate magnate)

My father taught me to work; he did not teach me to love it.

—Abraham Lincoln, 1809–1865
(U.S. president)

To this day I'm an early riser. That comes from Dad always saying "Off and on," meaning: Off your ass and on the deck. He didn't like us lying around; we had to be productive. . . .

I remember a time when I was eight years old and my dad sent me out to the drugstore to buy him some Neapolitan ice cream. He always loved Neapolitan. Gave me a quarter, just like always, because that's what a pint of Neapolitan cost in the early fifties.

I took the quarter and ran. I ran everywhere as a kid, especially when I was running an errand for my dad. I got to the drugstore and found they were out of Neapolitan. I was eight, remember. All of a sudden, the ice cream was the most important thing in the world, because

I hated ever telling Dad I couldn't get a job done for
him.

Then I did something fairly sharp for an eight-year-
old.

I ran across the street to the Mobil gas station on the
corner of Greenwood and Glenside Avenues. A friend
of my dad's, Bob Bradshaw, owned it. I went into his
office, out of breath, and asked if I could borrow fifty cents.

"What's the emergency, Reggie?" he asked.

I babbled something quickly about the ice cream,
and how I had to buy more for my dad than I thought,
and how I'd pay him back.

Bob Bradshaw gave me the money. I went back to the
drugstore. I used the extra fifty cents to buy a pint of
vanilla, a pint of chocolate, and a pint of strawberry.

The free enterprise system at work (I've always had a
flair for good business): Instant Neapolitan.

I hustled back home with the three pints of ice cream
and set them on the kitchen table. My dad just smiled
this great smile—an understanding smile—and asked me
how I'd managed.

"You owe Bob Bradshaw fifty cents," I said, chest
still pounding pretty good.

He reached into his pocket, gave me the money and said,
"Now git." I did, running back to the Mobil station, feeling
like a million bucks instead of fifty cents every step
of the way. I'd learned how to get the job done.

—REGGIE JACKSON

*

He was like the Zen teacher who gives his student a sharp
tap with cane, but doesn't embark on a great deal of
explanation.

—TONY HUSTON
(*director, son of* JOHN HUSTON)

*

My father was a restless and inventive man who was
always trying new things. He was the first person in town
to buy a motorcycle—an old Harley-Davidson, which he

rode through the dirt streets of our small city.
Unfortunately, my father and his motorcycle didn't get
along too well. He fell off it so often that he finally got
rid of it. As a result, he never again trusted any vehicle
with less than four wheels.

Because of that damn motorcycle, I wasn't allowed
to have a bicycle when I was growing up. Whenever I wanted
to ride a bike, I had to borrow one from a friend. On the
other hand, my father let me drive a car as soon as
I turned sixteen. This made me the only kid in
Allentown who went straight from a tricycle to a Ford. . . .

Once I was in Palm Springs for a meeting and I invited
my father to come out for a brief vacation. When the
meeting was over, a couple of us went out to play golf.
Although my father had never been on a golf course in
his life, we asked him to come along.

As soon as he hit the ball, he began to chase after
it—seventy years old and running all the way. I had
to keep reminding him: "Pop, slow down. Golf is a game
of walking!"

But that was my father for you. He always preached:
"Why walk when you can run?"

—LEE IACOCCA *(auto executive)*

I have often reproached myself for not publishing immediately
after Renoir's death selections from the many conversations
I had with him. But now I no longer regret it. The
passing of the years and my own later experiences have
given me a cleaner view of him. And there is one aspect
of him which I did not even glimpse at that period and
that is his genius. I admired his painting intensely, but
it was a blind sort of admiration. To tell the truth I was
totally ignorant of what painting was. I was hardly aware
of what art in general was all about. Of the world itself,
all I could take in was its outward appearances. Youth
is materialistic. Now I know that great men have no
other function in life than to help us to see beyond
appearances: to relieve us of some of the burden of matter—
to "unburden" ourselves, as the Hindus would say.

For Renoir, there were no petty or great events, no

minute or major artists, no small or great discoveries. There were animals, men, stones, and trees, which fulfilled their functions, and creatures that didn't. The chief function of a human being is to live; his first duty is to have a respect for life. These reflections were not intended to represent a philosophy: rather, they formed a part of the practical advice given by a father to his son. He used personal examples by way of illustration: "I had to shell green peas and I loathed it. But I knew that it was part of life. It I hadn't shelled the peas, my father would have had to, and he would not have been able to deliver on time the suit he was making for his customer, and the earth would have stopped turning, much to the shame of Galileo. . . ."

—JEAN RENOIR *(film director, son of painter* CLAUDE RENOIR)

John Lennon once told his son, Julian, that when he died, he would try to contact him by floating a white feather across a room. With that in mind, Julian wrote the song, "Well, I Don't Know."

It is about looking for signs of afterlife from Dad. . . . When I'm on my own, worried or scared, I just think about him a lot, you know. I almost talk to myself. For a while I was looking for some sign or something strange, but I'm not looking for it anymore. I believe if you look too much, you may not find it.

—JULIAN LENNON *(son of The Beatles'* JOHN LENNON)

I came from a town where there was a lot of anti-Semitism, and my father taught me to take care of myself. He always said, "If somebody takes advantage of you, you gotta do what you gotta do." In those days, you went out and settled it. There weren't guns, so you didn't worry about getting killed. You'd get your nose broken or whatever. There was a sense of honor.

I'm grateful for his sense of values, sense of fair play.
I'm grateful that I picked that up from him. But I think
more than anything else was the sense that he always trusted
me and always encouraged me and made me feel like I
was the best, even though there were many times when
I wasn't the best. I'm grateful for the fact that he gave
me an ego. He was never critical of me or my two sisters.
Obviously there were times when all of us disappointed
him in one way or another, but I never heard him
criticize me. He never asked, "Why can't you do better?"

—BUD YORKIN
(TV director and producer)

On the day the Krakow ghetto was finally liquidated, March
13, 1943, my father woke me before dawn. Taking me to
Plac Zgody, to a blind spot just behind the SS guardhouse,
he coolly snipped the barbed wire with a pair of pliers.
He gave me a quick hug, and I slipped through the fence
for the last time. Stefan had to stay behind with the other
children; there was no one to take him in on a
permanent basis.

When I got to the Wilks's, however, the door was locked.
No one was home. I wandered around for a while, uncertain
what to do. Then, glad of any excuse to rejoin my father,
I headed back to the ghetto.

Just short of the bridge I saw a column of male prisoners
being marched away by Germans with guns at the ready.
They were the last surviving inmates of the ghetto, and
among them was my father.

He didn't see me at first. I had to trot to keep up. The
marching men were attracting plenty of attention; many
people turned to stare. Still trotting, I tried to catch my
father's eye.

At last he spotted me.

I gestured, turning an imaginary key to illustrate my
predicament.

He dropped back two or three ranks with the tacit
assistance of others in the squad, unobtrusively changing
places with them so as to be farther from the nearest guard

and closer to me. Then, out of the corner of his mouth, he hissed, "Shove off!"

Those two brusque words stopped me in my tracks. I watched the column recede, then turned away. I didn't look back.

—ROMAN POLANSKI *(film director)*

II
REGRETS

Missed Opportunities

Every generation
Blames the one before
And all of their frustrations
Come beating on your door.
I know that I'm a prisoner
To all my father held so dear
I know that I'm a hostage
To all his hopes and fears
I just wish I could have told him
In the living years.

—MIKE RUTHERFORD
(from "The Living Years")

🍃

December 5, 1936
   Today is my father's birthday. He'd be eighty-six, if he'd
lived. I always wished he'd lived to see me elected to
this place. There'd have been no holding him.
                    —PRESIDENT HARRY S TRUMAN, 1884-1972
                              (in a letter to his wife, Bess)

🍃

It's a source of great sadness to me that my father died
without having seen me do anything worthwhile. He was

constantly having to make excuses for me. I loved him
and miss him very much.

—DANIEL DAY-LEWIS
(actor, son of C. DAY-LEWIS,
poet laureate of England)

❧

I have just one father. I want to make peace with him.
—MARVIN GAYE, 1939–1984
(singer, of his father, MARVIN GAY, SR.,
*who shot him to death
during a quarrel)*

❧

It is impossible, too, to avoid intense fits of recalling the
past. Such bouts are mercilessly penetrating in their self-
questioning; when did I ever have the guts to confront
my father about anything, to tell him his attitudes were
stupid, childish, wrong, sometimes close to being wicked
in their dangerous prejudices and ignorance? I remember
his once declaring with the firmness of blind faith that
Bernard Shaw was the reincarnation of the Devil! (I had
been in a couple of Shaw plays by this time and pretended
not to hear.) I thought back in envious admiration of my
sister's complete fearlessness of him; she would oppose
him directly; her brilliant eyes staring into his, she
would blaze. Her feebler brothers offered her no support—just
a weak, deprecating, "Oh, I say, Baba . . . that's a bit . . . ,"
to avoid a row at any cost.

—SIR LAURENCE OLIVIER, 1907–1989 *(actor)*

❧

When he was in the hospital, after his stroke, we all had
our private moments with him to say what we needed to
say. Although he was morphined up he would respond
to the best of his ability, by squeezing your hand or
somehow acknowledging what you had to say. It was
hard to tell how much he understood, but I let it flow and
it was cleansing. I wanted him to know that I loved him.

In the last three or so years we had made amends, but
there was a somewhat protracted period after he and
my mother broke up when our relationship was pretty
strained. From that standpoint it was important for me
to tell him that even though that had happened it was
sad, but through it all I loved him, shortcomings and
all. It was important for me to articulate that. I don't know
if he understood or not.

He was of a generation that didn't say, "I love you."
He just said, "Me and you baby." He'd say, "I love you"
to my sisters, but not to me and my brothers. He was a
hard guy without being a hard*ened* guy. I think he was
a byproduct of his times, and they were macho times.
So the sensitivity of kissing your sons wasn't there.
We were shaking his hand from the time we were twelve.
It wasn't physical. The generation that came after us is
much more physical. You see fathers kissing their sons
at ten, twelve, fifteen, twenty-eight, fifty. But it was
an unmanly thing to do in the macho directions of my
dad's generation.

—ED ECKSTINE

*

There's a card that sits on my desk that I look at every
day. I bought it for my dad the last Father's Day before
he died. I never sent it to him.

I bought the card about a month before Father's Day.
I really wanted to be on top of things and get it sent because
I was thinking about him all the time. He was in a nursing
home out in Colorado and I was in the East. I missed
him terribly.

The card reads "From Your Son," on the front, with a
simple painting of a boat on water like a child might do.
I think it evoked a favorite memory I have of him
coloring pictures with my daughter when she was about
six years old. Inside it reads:

> *It's difficult to tell you*
> *just how much you mean,*
> *because with every day*

you still mean more.
Happy Father's Day

I usually get blank cards and write my own message, but for some reason this moved me. So I bought it and stuck it in my bag. Then I just never never never sent it. I never even wrote on it.

That card reminds me every day that you should do the things you need to do while you're living. Don't wait and let the time pass. If you procrastinate you may not get it done.

In retrospect, I'm glad I have the card. It reminds me of something very strong I felt about my father and makes me appreciate more the time when he was around. Maybe my not sending it was a way of keeping him here forever.

—FRANKIE FAISON

When my brother died of cancer in 1966 at age thirty-nine, my father began a grieving process that lasted almost twenty-five years. During that time he suffered from chronic, debilitating headaches that could not be cured. At one point, a doctor tried to tell him that his headaches were related to his grief, but he persisted in treating the pain as a medical problem, and the torment continued. After my father's death at eighty-six, I thought about how he could have been helped.

—BILL MOYERS *(journalist)*

My father did not complain. He kept busy observing the people around him . . . and their touching, sometimes humorous foibles. . . . He also spoke of me: "When you were at the university, you said that uncovering the secrets of nature could make you happy. We don't choose our fate, but I'm sorry that yours took a different turn; I imagine you could have been happier."

I don't remember my reply. I think I agreed that we don't choose our fate. What more could I have said to

him on that November day in 1961? The twists and turns
in my life that might have cheered him—or pained him—still
lay in the future. I couldn't tell him about the latest
test [of the bombs Sakharov worked on] nor would
it have been to the point. I couldn't even share my concern
about the dangers of testing. He knew my papers on the
peaceful use of thermonuclear energy, and he was proud
of them. But they weren't enough to allay his
misgivings. The one thing I might have said to cheer him
up was that I intended to work seriously on theoretical
physics and cosmology, but that wasn't yet clear in my
own mind. And I didn't want to believe that these
conversations would be our last ones. I was wrong, although
my mistake was a common one.

> —ANDREI SAKHAROV, 1921–1989
> *(Russian Nobel laureate physicist
> and human rights activist)*

When I came home that night [when his father, singer
Ricky Nelson, was killed in a plane crash], I was so frightened
that my dad wasn't going to be there in his bathrobe
anymore, that he wasn't going to come off the road
again. So my brother Gunnar and I got an apartment the
next day because we couldn't stand to live there.

> —MATTHEW NELSON
> *(son of singer* RICKY NELSON)

I once said, in a would-be casual aside in an interview
many years ago, that my father had only read one book
in his life, and that, I think, was by Hall Caine. Such
a remark, in an English class situation, appears to imply
some kind of condescension or patronizing contempt, which
was not the case at all. My father was very proud of the
fact that I seemed to be bright and could draw and write.
He used to put some of my drawings up on the
mantelpiece, and then tear them up if he thought I was
getting too uppity. He himself, when describing the past,
would almost casually describe the color of the sky and

how he felt that day. And he would always draw an apple or something on the white margins of the newspaper.

Of course, the English class system—I don't mean British, because it's not the same in Scotland and Wales—is so strong, so innate, instinctive almost. I grew up in a wholly enclosed coal mining community, which is geographically isolated as well; in sophisticated metropolitan terms you could even call it "backward." At school I was very good at exams. I had a high IQ, and teachers who, although they weren't class traitors, tried to inculcate us with a love of reading books and of learning, and so I started to pull away—willy-nilly, I began the process of judging my background. Then that terrible English thing creeps in at the edges—a kind of complicated shame about the way you speak, the fact that there are no books in the house, and you make assumptions about your family. You are too young to deal with that, but the guilt comes much later. When I started writing Dad was still alive—I was living about ten miles away on the edges of the Forest of Dean—and I think he got to the stage where he was shy with me: he would lean on the door-jamb when I was in the middle of something and say, "Bist thou all right, old butt?" And I'd say, "Yes, thank you, Dad." And he'd hover a bit and say, "Well, good to see thou at work." It's too late, but if only I could now say, "Come on in. Just let me put my pen away. Let us talk."

—Dennis Potter
*(British playwright, novelist,
and filmmaker)*

My father was a doctor and his brothers were in music, as I am. I don't know if that's why, but he never complimented me to my face. He never indicated that he thought my work was worth anything. I hear from other people how proud he was of me. It was a funny kind of thing.

—Randy Newman *(singer)*

He died of a sudden heart attack when I was ten. I would
have said to him stop smoking. If I knew what I knew
now, I would have made him stop smoking. I'd have
said, "You don't know what's coming. You'll live a lot
longer." I had bypass surgery in '87; if they'd had that
then, maybe he would have lived. Although I don't know
because he did keel over and die.

I wish he could have seen all that happened to his son.
I pinch myself everyday at all the good things that have
happened to me. It would have been nice to have him
see his grandchildren, my brother's kids, and all that's
happened to me. His two sons turned out pretty well. My
brother's a lawyer, he's vice president of a big pharmaceutical
company. My mother lived a long and happy life and
she died when she was seventy-seven.

He'd probably be most proud of the people I've met and
the respect I've garnered and the fact that I've been able
to be at the White House and ask presidents questions.
He was an immigrant. This was a guy who couldn't
speak English when he came here when he was nineteen,
and his son is on national television. I think he'd be proud
that I'm seen where he was born. He could go to his
village and I'd be seen.

I wish he'd seen me at my bar mitzvah. And getting an
honorary degree two weeks ago at Pratt in Brooklyn, since
I never went to college, having them put that cap and
gown on me and speaking to the graduates. Being the
commencement speaker at Columbia University medical
school. I would like for him to have been there when my
daughter was born. I would have liked to have laughed
at him when the Dodgers beat the Yankees, because
he was a Yankee fan. I don't know why he was a Yankee
fan. Probably because they were named Yankees. He loved
America. He had the flag in front of his store.

—LARRY KING

❧

I wish my father had been here to share the first time
I played Carnegie Hall, the first time my son started

playing with me. Or the first time my daughters started
singing with me, which was at Carnegie Hall in 1992—
those kinds of family things. He is still missed. And
then there are the larger issues of what's going on in the
world today. I would have loved to have seen and been
able to see his reaction to the way the world is, and
to know how he would have changed and adapted to this
environment.

—ARLO GUTHRIE

I was very close with my father, but I miss that we didn't
share actually telling each other how much we loved each
other. I think I never expressed that in words. I kissed
my father until I was forty-five or fifty. He died at
eighty. We were physical enough. But neither one of us
was ever able to say it to each other. As I grow older, I
wish I'd had the opportunity.

—BUD YORKIN

I sort of wish I could talk to my parents. I find myself
wanting to show them the world as it is now, and ask them
what do they think of their actions. You look back at
the fifties and at all that has changed—Ronald Reagan
kissing babies in Red Square. I hope they would feel it
was worth it.

—ROBERT MEEROPOL
(son of JULIUS and ETHEL ROSENBERG,
who were executed in 1953 for
allegedly spying for the Soviet Union)

He'll see no more Times Square
honky-tonk movie marquees, bus stations at midnight
Nor the orange sun ball
rising thru treetops east toward New York's skyline
His velvet armchair facing the window will be empty

*He won't see the moon over house roofs
or sky over Paterson's streets.*

New York, February 26, 1976
—ALLEN GINSBERG

❧

If I could have one wish, it would be to turn back the clock
and take away all the pain Dad had to endure.

—JOE NIEKRO
(pro baseball pitcher)

❧

I remember one time I went to see *Field of Dreams* with
my best buddy. We sat there camouflaged in the dark and
in the quiet. There is this scene where Kevin Costner
is able to say everything he needed to say to his dad
by asking him to play catch. Costner gets a second chance
to say, "I'm sorry and I love you." After all those years
he gets his say.

I came to this with my buddy and we were swept away
with the scene. After all these years I wanted my say. We
were sitting next to one another and he was right next to
his father—who is an aloof man, who didn't do things
like that with his son. And my dad was dead. I gripped
my buddy's hand tightly and tears rolled down our unmeasured
faces. I wouldn't have believed it when my father was here,
but somebody recently told me that he cried in movies,
too. It doesn't matter, I suppose, that they couldn't name
the movie or movies where they saw him cry.

—KEITH ORCHARD *(fiction writer)*

❧

You know, since my father died, it's been a lot different.
I feel a lot more ambitious. It really does something to you
when your father passes away. Takes a while to get
over it too. I got a new perspective on life.

—BRIAN WILSON
(singer with THE BEACH BOYS)

I *never had a chance to talk to him, and I still feel—kind of temporary about myself.*

—Willy Loman
(*from* Death of a Salesman)

❦

There was the blinding heat of the glass factory; a roaring hell of fiery furnaces where the condemned, half-naked bodies gleaming, made bottles, bottles, bottles. There was a hierarchy in the skills of the damned. On top, the bellows-lunged blower arced his tube—tipped with a white-hot blob—from furnace to form; then into the tube, gargoylish cheeks ballooning, he blew and blew and blew.

Below the blower—the form-man. He tapped the blob in jaws of iron, then untrapped, red-hot, the bottle. Next down the totem pole—the short-paddler. With bottle on paddle he fed the hot mouth of the annealing over. Below them all was the long-paddler. Papa was a long-paddler.

I brought him lunch as a child and watched him running, like a pole-vaulter running, back arched backward; running, bare-waisted, sweated to the bone, clutching one end of a twenty-foot paddle balancing the weight of six dull-red bottles.

My heart ached for him. Papa, illiterate Papa, ignorant of language and laws; running, dreaming of farms, running, lungs burning, from oven to oven; ten hours a day six days a week, a long-paddler running—for twelve lousy dollars. For this he came to America?

—FRANK CAPRA, 1897-1971
(*film director*)

❦

I managed to labor out two short detective stories. With the slender proceeds from these, my wife and children returned to Nebraska for a visit and I caught a bus for New York. . . . We arrived in Oklahoma City the third day out, and I laid over there a day to see Pop. He could not believe it was I when I first walked in on him. The seven long, lonely months must have seemed like years to him, and I think he had begun to feel we had abandoned him.

I made him understand the truth: that his remaining here was due to circumstances beyond our control.

"Well, it's all over now," he said. "You just help me get my things together, and I'll clear out of here right now."

"Pop," I said. "I—"

"Well?" He looked at me. "You're going to take me away, aren't you? That's why you've come back?"

I hesitated. Then, I said, yes, that was why. "But I can't go with you, Pop. I'm on my way to New York."

"Oh?" He frowned troubledly. "Well, I guess I could travel by myself if—"

"I've got a swell job there," I lied. "Give me a—Well, just give me a month and I can send you to California by stateroom. Get you a nurse if you need one. But the best I can do now is a bus ticket."

"I don't know," he said dubiously. "I'm afraid to doctor . . . I'm afraid I couldn't . . ." He sat back down on the bed. "You're sure, Jimmie? If I wait another month, you'll—"

"That's a promise. And I never break a promise."

I started across town toward my rooming house, worrying again—continuing to worry. It was a day short of five weeks since I had left Oklahoma. Not much over a month, to be sure, but to an old man, a lonely old man who secretly feared that he might be forsaken . . .

I reached Fifth Avenue. Instead of crossing it, I suddenly turned and headed uptown. Surely the publisher would be able to make his decision by this time. By God, he simply *had* to.

Well, he had.

He walked me into his office, his arm around my shoulders. "Got some good reports from Louis and Dick. They're going to fix us up with blurbs to put on the cover. . . . Now, I do feel that quite a few revisions are necessary. There are a couple of chapters I'd like to see excised, and new ones substituted. But—"

"Oh," I said, pretty drearily. "Then it'll still be quite a while before—"

"What? Oh, no, we'll pay you for it right now. We're

definitely accepting it. Incidentally, when you get this one out of the way, we'll be glad to—Yes?"

The receptionist was standing in the doorway. She murmured an apology, held out a yellow Western Union envelope. "This came in yesterday, Mr. Thompson. I tried to reach you by phone, but—"

"It must be from my mother," I said. "I wasn't sure how long I'd be at that rooming house, so I told her to—to—"

I ripped the envelope open.

I stared down at the message.

Blindly. Stricken motionless.

"Bad news?" The publisher's hushed voice.

"My father," I said. "He died two days ago."

—JIM THOMPSON
(writer of noir crime thrillers)

My father died just as I became an adult. . . . It's a tough thing because you've kind of known this guy as a child and then, just at the point where you start to understand where he's coming from, he's gone. So now you look back and he almost becomes a mythical person to you.

—JOE MANTEGNA *(actor)*

Clashes

He used to coach baseball in the Little League and I used
to pitch. One day I'd thrown a football the day before and
I couldn't get the ball over the plate. It threw me off.
I must have walked ten guys. And I cried. The first
time I brought my second wife there to meet him, he told
her that story. And he told it three times. The most
humiliating incident of my childhood.

My brother thinks he was competitive with me, but
I don't know. I raced him one time. He was fast. He was
the New York City forty-yard champ in the Public School
Athletic League. I was around thirteen. Now I race my
own kids, and even when I could beat them, I let them
beat me. But I raced him and I was fast then. We were
running, and I was looking at him, and he was looking
at me, and I couldn't beat him. He wouldn't let me beat
him. He was looking right at me and smiling, and he
just wouldn't let me beat him.

—RANDY NEWMAN

My daddy, he tickles me. He says, "Don't listen to the
others, boy; I made you." He says he made me because
he fed me vegetable soup when I was a baby, going
without shoes to pay the food bill. Well, he's my father
and I guess more teenagers ought to realize what they
owe their folks. But listen here. When you want to talk
about who made me, you talk to me. Who made me
is me.

—MUHAMMAD ALI
(former heavyweight champion)

51

It was a blessing and a curse at the same time to have
Woody Guthrie for a father. People would come to hear
me because I was Woody Guthrie's son, but if they
didn't hear what they wanted to they were more
disappointed. There are a lot of people who are still upset
with me because I don't ride freight trains or support some
of the things he supported. But the world has changed,
and I know that if he were here today, if there were
battles to be fought between us, we'd still be fighting them.
                                                    —ARLO GUTHRIE

*

There were many times when I wished that I had been
born into a different family, a plain and simple family of
impeccable American credentials—a no-secrets,
nonwhispering, no-enemy-soldiers family that never
received mail from POW camps, or prayed to a painting
of an ugly monk, or ate Italian bread with pungent cheese.
    . . . I would have welcomed a father who could have
become more relaxed and casual, and who on weekends
would have removed his vest and tie and played ball with
me on the beach or in the small park across from the
Methodist Tabernacle church. But this last wish, I knew,
was pure fantasy on my part—I had made the discovery
the summer before, after I had spent a half-hour bouncing
a red rubber ball against a brick wall in the parking lot
behind our shop . . .
    I assumed that my father was away from the store
having lunch, as he always did in the middle of Saturday
afternoons; I was therefore suddenly shaken by the sight
of him opening the back door, then walking toward me
with a frown on his face. Not knowing what to do, but
nonetheless compelled by nervous energy to do something,
I quickly took the ball in my right hand, cocked my arm,
and threw it at him.
    The ball soared forty feet in a high arc toward his
head. He was so startled to see it coming that he halted
his step and stared skittishly up at the sky through his
steel-rimmed glasses. Then—as if not knowing whether

to block the ball or try to catch it—he extended his arms upward and cupped his soft tailor's hands, and braced himself for the impact.

I stood watching anxiously from the far corner of the lot, no less shocked than he that I had chosen this moment to confront him—perhaps for the first time in his life—with the challenge of catching a ball. I cringed as I saw the ball hit him solidly on the side of the neck, carom off a shoulder, rebound against the wall behind him, and come rolling slowly back to his feet, where it finally stopped.

As I waited, holding my breath, he lowered his head and began to rub his neck. Then, seeing the ball at his feet, he stooped to pick it up. For a moment he held the rubber ball in his right hand and examined it as if it were a strange object. He squeezed it. He turned it around in his fingers. Finally, with a bashful smile, he turned toward me, cocked his arm awkwardly, and tried to throw the ball in my direction.

But it slipped from his grip, skidded weakly at an oblique angle, and rolled under one of his dry-cleaning trucks parked along the edge of the lot.

As I hastened to retrieve it, I saw him shrug his shoulders. He seemed to be very embarrassed. He who cared so much about appearances had tried his best, and yet the results were pitiful. It was a sorrowful moment for both of us.

—GAY TALESE
(writer, on his Italian-born father,
an assimilated American)

When I began psychoanalysis . . . I discovered that my mother hardly appeared [in my dreams] at all—the ogres and lions and kidnappers led by association to my father and other father figures. This is in accord with Freud's observation that the most basic rivalry—and most subtle fear—is what the son feels toward his father, mainly in his unconscious mind.

—DR. BENJAMIN SPOCK
(physician and author)

Like most American boys I didn't just love my father. I wanted to admire and look up to him too. And that was difficult, because my father was a failure, and, as I came to realize later, not particularly ashamed of it either. For instance, anyone who puts down his occupation as a hotel night clerk is acknowledging that he has no ambition for a start. And that's how my father described himself—as a night clerk. It's like admitting you're a mouse and only dare to come out after dark and snuffle around for cheese.

—DARRYL F. ZANUCK
(Hollywood tycoon)

He was a very scary person to me. I wasn't a shy little kid hovering in a corner or anything, but I did find his presence overwhelming. I was always aware of my father's need to compete and dominate everyone with whom he came in contact.

Then came this fateful night I'll never forget. I guess I was fourteen and partly because of my father's inspiration, and because I was so eager to emulate him, I'd become a pretty good athlete. I'd also started playing around with girls, and I guess my father must have seen me doing—well, you know what randy kids get up to when they have a pretty chick around. Anyway, this night the movie [he was screening] was a clunker and as usual we started fooling around on the couch. And as we wrestled, I could just feel, for the first time, that perhaps I was as strong as he was. Well, suddenly, I got him in a perfect headlock. And I began to squeeze. I played it just as he did, and I showed him no mercy. His face became all red, and his eyes were almost bulging out of their sockets and I thought, Hey, this guy is going to die if he doesn't give up! But I just kept up! I just kept squeezing, and I could hear a voice saying over and over what he had asked me to do over all these years. And it wasn't until he finally blurted out "Give!" that I realized it had been my voice which had been giving him the ultimatum—and my God, I had beaten him! It gave me no pleasure at all, the moment I saw his face. This

was my father, for Christ's sake, the invulnerable man!
I just wished it had never happened. It was just the
way he looked at me. It wasn't nice at all. I still loved my
father, but suddenly, everything was different—and maybe
I didn't admire him so much anymore.

Incidentally, from that time on, he never wanted to
wrestle on the couch anymore. I mean he didn't specifically
say: "Let's not do it anymore." It just never happened.

—RICHARD ZANUCK *(son of* DARRYL F. ZANUCK)

Old man, I loved you as only your son could. The whole
world admired you, but I admired you more. "Yul Brynner's
son": for years this mixed blessing was the central fact
of my existence. Truly, I have been among the most
fortunate people ever born, but I could not survive as an
appendage of your persona, and therefore I was bound
to disappoint you. For that you never really forgave
me. Forgiveness was never exactly your forte. Suffering
fools gladly was not your specialty, either, and much of
my life I have been a fool—I freely confess that at the outset.

You regarded your only son as the extension of your
own soul into the next generation; when I was a child,
you loved me the same way you loved yourself. But when
it came time to tear myself free from your kingdom, it seemed
to you as if your own right arm was rebelling against
your authority. I could not hope to survive without an
identity—not sober, anyway. Neither could I inherit your
power, for we must each make our own.

—ROCK BRYNNER

Although my father had expressed his intolerance of this
sexual persuasion [homosexuality] I certainly experimented
with it, briefly and unsuccessfully, pressured as much
by curiosity as by others to explore this classical ideal.
It was not for me. Subsequently, though, many of my dearest
friends were homosexual and I was given many professional
opportunities to understand and portray their kind. I
decided to stop kissing my father, although in retrospect

I deplore the curtailment of this intimacy. Then, however, a masculine-man-to-man handshake seemed to be more consonant with the new maturity. We became friendly rivals waging bets on the most abstruse subjects such as whether a plane existed capable of carrying a bus. I won. On aerial matters I was usually invincible.

—MICHAEL YORK *(actor)*

When you are living under the shadow of a great oak tree, the small sapling, so close to the parent tree, does not perhaps receive enough sunshine.

—RANDOLPH CHURCHILL
(only son of Winston Churchill)

I was always some sort of curiosity. And it affected the normal relations between a father and son, making it doubly difficult for me to establish my own identity. . . . Dad himself was a terrifying figure to a small boy. He was powerfully built—in West Point he could chin himself five times with his right hand and three times with his left—and in his youth had literally lived for athletics. I could never measure up to these standards, try as I might. I participated in all sports available at [school] and suppose that I was probably of average caliber. But Dad could never understand why I was not a star. The fact is that I was always painfully thin; Dad wrote from [his military post in] the Philippines when I was fourteen that I had to reach the weight of ninety-two pounds before I could play football. I stuffed myself on bananas and drank about a gallon of water one night before weighing in.

—JOHN S.D. EISENHOWER
(son of former President
DWIGHT D. EISENHOWER)

To have dreamed of my father's death on the eve of that second MRI wasn't at all remarkable, nor, really, was the

incarnation that the dream had worked upon his body.
I lay in bed till it was light, thinking of all the family
history compressed into that snippet of silent dream-
film: just about every major theme of his life was encapsulated
there, everything of significance to both of us, starting
with his immigrant parents' transatlantic crossing in
steerage, extending to his grueling campaign to get
ahead, the battle to make good against so many obstructive
forces—as a poor boy robbed of serious schooling, as a
Jewish working man in the Gentile insurance colossus—
and ending with his transformation, by the brain tumor,
into an enfeebled wreck. . . .

Then one night some six weeks later, at around
4:00 a.m., he came in a hooded white shroud to reproach
me. He said, "I should have been dressed in a suit.
You did the wrong thing." I awakened screaming. All that
peered out from the shroud was the displeasure in his dead
face. And his only words were a rebuke: I had dressed
him for eternity in the wrong clothes.

—PHILIP ROTH *(American writer)*

❧

I was summoned to the upstairs sitting room, where I found
my father pacing. He began in peremptory fashion.

"Your mother is troubled by your relationship with the
Beck girl."

"Yes sir."

"She's spoken to you about it?"

"Yes sir."

"Then why do you persist?"

"I like her."

There was a pause while he digested this. Obviously the
problem wasn't going to be simple. Finally, he said,
"That's reasonable enough—but we can't have you
worrying your mother."

"No sir."

(Don't let those "sirs" fool you. In more casual
moments I called him "Dad," but this was a formal
occasion calling for "sir." If the ax was to fall, he'd have
to wield it and there'd be no higher appeal.)

"What do you suggest be done about it?"

"I don't know, sir."

"She's three years your senior. Can't you find friends among your own age group?"

"Yes sir—but I can't find her."

I think my father was about to smile, but he resisted it and maintained a sternly judicial manner.

"Very well. Are you seeing her today?"

"We're playing tennis—sir."

"Well, from now on, you are not to see her"—I held my breath—"more than once a day. If you are playing tennis with her in the afternoon you are not taking her dancing in the evening. If you are spending the evening with her, you are not to play tennis with her in the afternoon. Is that clear?"

"Yes sir."

And the interview was over. As far as I remember it was our one and only confrontation. I remember it with great affection and delight.

—HUME CRONYN
(actor whose father, HUME CRONYN, SR.,
was a member of the
Canadian Parliament)

The fundamental defect of fathers is that they want their children to be a credit to them.

—BERTRAND RUSSELL, 1872–1972
(British philosopher)

My father was dark, ruddy, with a fine laugh. He was a coal miner. He was one of the sanguine temperament, warm & hearty, but unstable: he lacked principle, as my mother would have said. He deceived her & lied to her. She despised him—he drank.

. . . I was born hating my father: as early as ever I can remember. I shivered with horror when he touched me. He was very bad before I was born.

—D. H. LAWRENCE, 1872–1930
(British author)

I can't even imagine a father who is nice or kind or good.
Whenever I think of a child, I always think of somebody
afraid. Whenever I think of a wife, I always think of somebody
afraid. I'll never be writing about the Waltons or a
Cosby-like family, because they simply did not exist
in my universe. And once you've had a childhood like mine,
I don't think you quite get over it. . . .

I had this father with a single-digit IQ and the
musculature of an orangutan in my childhood. Because
of him I grew up hating Ireland, and Irish Catholics—and
I didn't even know any besides him. To me, to be Irish
is to beat your children, drink too much, to be stupid
about religions, get maudlin on St. Patrick's day. That
day is when Dad used to get drunk—it's always been like
Kristallnacht to me.

—PAT CONROY *(author)*

We hated each other. We hated each other so much that
other feelings didn't get enough light. It disfigured me.
When I think of [home] I have to search for the faces
of my friends, their voices, the rooms where I was made
welcome. But I can always see Dwight's [my stepfather's]
face and hear his voice. I hear his voice in my own when
I speak to my children in anger. They hear it too, and
look at me in surprise. My youngest once said, "Don't
you love me anymore?"

—TOBIAS WOLFF *(writer)*

I look at my opponent and I see my dad. So I have to take
him out. I have to kill him.

—JAMES TONEY
*(middleweight boxer whose father
abused his mother and left when
he was young)*

I wish that my relationship with Dad had been such that I could have gone into his office, put my feet up and shared thoughts with him about the future of IBM. By about 1950 I thought I'd learned the business. I understood what we were doing, . . . knew where I wanted IBM to go. But Dad wasn't finished with me yet. I was still only executive vice president, and he made it pretty clear that if I wanted more responsibility I was going to have to keep fighting him for it every step of the way. Once when I complained of his rough treatment Dad growled, "I don't have a lot of time to teach you and I'm doing it the only way I know how." He was determined not to stop until he had tested me, tempered me, and forged me in his image.

Dad and I would usually meet toward the end of the day, after I had been working tremendously hard. He'd only really get going around five o'clock at night, which was the time I'd want to catch my train to Greenwich. But the buzzer would buzz and there I'd be, fagged, and Dad would say, "I'm going to send Farwell to Kalamazoo," which would be exactly the opposite of what we'd agreed on the day before.

I'd say, "Dad, you know, we really talked that through and we decided it wasn't a very good thing to send Farwell to Kalamazoo."

"Well, I've thought about it further and I've changed my mind."

"But I already told Farwell that—"

"You shouldn't have done that!" he'd say, and we'd be off to the races.

Our worst fights were not at the office where outsiders might hear, but at my parents' townhouse on East Seventy-fifth street. If I had a late dinner in the city, or early meetings scheduled for the next day, I'd sometimes stay overnight with them rather than commute home to Greenwich. I'd sleep in the same bedroom that I had before the war. Looking back now, I'm not sure why I kept doing that. To my father, that opulent house represented everything he had ever aspired to in life; for me it just brought back memories of the unhappy years I lived there as an IBM salesman.

. . . It never made any difference that this might be something I'd worked on over a long period and just gotten resolved. "I'm not at all satisfied with the way it's being handled," he'd say, and there would go the whole wall that I'd laboriously put up brick by brick by brick, right down in my face. I loved the old boy and he knew it, but I didn't have the energy or time to rebuild walls he smashed down. I'd come out of a deep sleep and be in the middle of a battle in no time.

The best strategy would have been to let him blow himself out. Maybe if it had been 9:00 a.m. and I'd just come back from a week's vacation, I'd have been able to say, "Let me take another look at it." But usually I would come back at him hard, and we'd be in one hellacious fight. He'd get livid. His jowls would shake. All the old family tensions would come boiling out, and I'd let him have it with everything I had.

. . . It would frequently end in tears. Then Dad and I would hug—and go to bed frustrated. We'd swear we'd never do it gain, and within two or three weeks there would be another moment of difference which would escalate into another white-hot argument. It amazes me that two people could torture each other to the degree Dad and I did and not call it quits.

. . . Dad was constantly trying to change me, and I was trying to change him. I wanted an easy old-shoe pal and he couldn't be that. He'd have liked me to be more pliant and defy him less. Each of us wanted something that the other couldn't give.

. . . In truth there wasn't much I could do, which is why those fights were so deeply disturbing. They were savage, primal, and unstoppable. My father loved me and wanted me to thrive; I loved him and wanted to see him live his life without trauma, without embarrassment, without strain to his health. But while I always tried to live up to his expectations, he was never satisfied, because no son can ever totally please his father. And when he criticized me I found it impossible to hold back my rage.

—Thomas J. Watson, Jr.
(son of Thomas J. Watson, Sr.,
founder of IBM)

What harsh judges fathers are to all young men!
                              —TERENCE, c. 190–159 B.C.
                                        (Roman dramatist)

🍂

The old man was a flamboyant editor and publisher. He
lived for headlines and national press battles. I lived in
my father's shadow all my life.
                        —WILLIAM R. HEARST, JR., 1908–1993
                            (newspaper editor and heir to Hearst
                         publishing empire, established by his father,
                                        WILLIAM R. HEARST, SR.*)*

🍂

I can't listen to my father forever. He can't direct my life
and career indefinitely. The cord should have been broken
years ago, but at thirty years old I was still on that show
[Ozzie and Harriet] saying "Hi Mom, Hi Pop" every
week.
                                        —DAVID NELSON
                        (actor, son of actor OZZIE NELSON)

🍂

I remember I got in a motorcycle accident once and I was
laid up in bed. My dad had a barber come in and cut my
hair and I can remember telling my dad I hated him
and I would never, ever forget it.

   He had been so disappointed, had so much stuff beaten
out of him . . . that he couldn't accept the idea that I had
a dream and I had possibilities. The things I wanted,
he thought were foolish.
                                        —BRUCE SPRINGSTEEN

🍂

He'd been doing it [heroin] for years. Not shooting but
snorting. I told him to get help. He didn't listen. When

they caught him, he said, "I'm Spike Lee's father! Spike's my son!" He gave me up to try and not spend the night in jail.

—SPIKE LEE *(actor, director)*

My old man made the Great Santini look like Leo Buscaglia.

—DENNIS MILLER *(comedian)*

I never forgave my father for being a bigot.

—NORMAN LEAR
(TV producer and creator of Archie Bunker)

Daddy was always criticizing me for the way I walked and talked and for the people I was running with. He would get real mad at me. He'd say, "My father had seven sons and I wanted seven sons. You've spoiled it, you're only half a son." And then he'd hit me. But I couldn't help it. That was the way I was.

—LITTLE RICHARD *(singer)*

I was flattered to go along on my father's religious missions. . . . The spirit enraptured me. The strength of my singing surprised me. That's how I found the courage to sing according to feeling. I let my voice do things choir teachers would never allow. . . . Sometimes I wondered, though, whether Father was jealous of my voice. At gospel meetings, for example, when I pleased all the women, he'd look at me like I'd done something very bad. He hated it when my singing won more praise than his sermons. . . .

When I left home to start my career, I wanted to tell Father that I wished never to see him again. I wanted to forget everything he'd done to me as a child, but that wasn't possible. We just looked at each other. I think we

were both afraid of what we might say. Father and I
had special ways of hurting each other. If I could have
spoken my heart, I'd have said "Please love me." But
I didn't say a word, and neither did he. . . .

All the time since [I became a recording artist], Father
and I had little to say to each other. It was still hard
for me to even look at him, even though I knew that
he'd been collecting articles on me for the last ten years.
He kept everything—more for his ego than mine.

—MARVIN GAYE

Silences

My father never has much to say to me, but I know he thinks about a lot of things. I know he's driving himself crazy thinking about these things. And yet he sure ain't got much to say when we sit down to talk.

—BRUCE SPRINGSTEEN

I was always trying to make conversation with him, which was difficult, because he didn't like to talk. He thought he was no good at it, which was not true. . . .

He was a man who felt awkward about life. He was embarrassed about having been married many times, he was embarrassed about giving us compliments. If he thought we were doing a good job, we would hear it from his agent. He was painfully shy around us. I wish I had read his biography years ago, because I didn't understand that until later. I thought I was a total failure—that there was nothing I could do to make my father appreciate anything about me. Not until his last three or four years could I force him to tell me he loved me.

—PETER FONDA
(son of actor HENRY FONDA*)*

My father and I did not talk much during dinner. It did not seem as if there were very much to talk about. After the meal he would lie on the couch and listen to the radio and read magazines and I would go into my room and play dice games. . . .

My father was not an active man. He was deaf in one ear, so he had not fought in the war. He did not exercise, he did not participate in any sports. Sometimes

he played gin rummy. Mostly, when he was not working
on specifications, or looking at his stamp collection, he
lay on the couch and listened to the radio and read
newspapers and magazines, and, once in a while, a
detective novel. He developed a pot belly and became
bald at an early age. He was a quiet man, clumsy when
trying to express affection. He would put his arm around
me at a football game and I'd resent it. I think that
because he had not had a father to grow up with, he
did not know how to be one very well. Fatherhood, I suspect,
seemed to him like a second language—one that he had
learned but not quite mastered.

—JOE MCGINNISS *(writer)*

*

Whenever I'm asked what kind of man my father was,
the words that come to mind are "grave but just." I was
in awe of him, but I knew I could trust him to be fair
and calm in any case of disapproval. . . .

My father went out of his way to be companionable with
me. Before I could read to myself, he read to me *Ten Boys
from History* and *The Man without a Country*. He
welcomed me when he was working on projects or
repairs in the cellar. Twice he took me on trips to investigate
prospective summer cottages in Maine, and once to New
York to hear the opera *Madame Butterfly*, which he
loved. He called me "Benno" to indicate friendliness.
Yet I still think of him simply as grave but just.

When my sisters are asked what Father was like, they
melt with affection and enthusiasm: "He was a darling!
He called us by pet names. He told us little stories. He
held our hands." Obviously, parents appear quite different
to different children, but particularly to children of different
sexes. In general mothers seem—and often are—more
critical of their daughters, as fathers seem to their sons,
though there are plenty of exceptions.

Three times in adolescence I felt I let my father down.
When he was away on business trips, he solemnly left
me in charge of the coal furnace; twice I let it go out
and once was unable to get it going again before he came
home. He discovered it dead and cold. He didn't scold or

reproach; he just looked at me sadly and I felt terrible. Another time, I borrowed the family car for the evening after a big football game, parked it in front of Longley's Restaurant, and forgot to lock it. When I came out, it was gone. I felt sick. I notified the police and went home to bed. When Father came in the next morning to wake me, I confessed, and again I interpreted his expression as disappointed. (Fortunately, the police found the car next morning with nothing amiss except an empty gas tank.)

Despite my awe of my father and my feeling of distance from him, I know he was the one who inspired by example and built in me the obligation to be fair and reasonable, to be dependable, to be self-controlled (even though it was often carried too far), and to be dignified.

—Dr. Benjamin Spock

*

He often played his violin in an effort to make us quiet. But I also recall my mother saying that even the loudest baby crying didn't seem to disturb Father. He would go on with his work completely impervious to noise. . . . Probably the only project he ever gave up on was me. He tried to give me advice, but he soon discovered that I was too stubborn and that he was wasting his time.

—Hans Albert Einstein
(son of Albert Einstein)

*

Most of the time my father would put a cool distance between himself and his emotions. That's the way a lot of policemen cope with the daily potential for disruption—and my father was particularly well-suited for this line of work. Unfortunately, he found it difficult to warm back up when he came home. I could come to him with problems, and he could cope with them—that's what he did all day—but it was a rare moment when I felt I was more than a professional case, when he made me feel he knew and cared that these were my feelings that were battered or my personal aches that needed soothing.

. . . It was made clear to me early on that books were
important, but often my father would rather read them than
talk to me. I would ask him a question or start a conversation,
and he wouldn't even acknowledge that I was there.
If I was asking something factual, he'd tell me to look
it up; if I kept after him, he'd get annoyed and chase me
away. There was no feeling in the world like asking your
father "Where does electricity come from?" and not
getting his eyes off the printed page. I wanted to know
about politics, machines, history—"Why is that like that?"—
but pretty soon I stopped asking. I learned the facts of
life, and almost everything else, out on the street.
    . . . Being an only child had its advantages. While
I missed out on an older brother to show me the ropes,
or a younger sister to torment, I did get my own room,
a fact that went a long way toward shaping my
personality. With such privacy I was unique among my
friends. My room was my sanctuary, where I would lick
my wounds after another sidewalk disaster or retreat to
read or daydream when no one else would talk to me.
It looked right out on the Cloisters, a medieval-period
stone monastery that the city had made into a park and
museum, and in my many monkish moments I could
manufacture the calm I needed. I grew up in that room,
from three years old through high school, and though
I outgrew the bed and bumped my head on the doorway,
it held all my secrets, and I had plenty.

—KAREEM ABDUL-JABBAR
(basketball champion, son of
FERDINAND LEWIS ALCINDOR,
*a musician classically trained
at Juilliard who became a police
officer to support his family)*

I took off my uniform and started for the showers, and
standing over at the far wall was my dad. He had been
there for 2½ hours and he had not come into my
cubicle. We locked eyes. He stood up straight and said
to me, "Hey, great game!" I burst into tears. Compliments
from my dad never had been easy coming, and I reached

out and we hugged each other. From that moment, I
knew my dad.

—MARK HARMON *(on his father,*
football legend TOM HARMON,
after a hard-won victory
for the UCLA Bruins in 1972.
A few years later, Mark bought
his dad a new Mercedes for Christmas.)

I remember one Memorial Day when I appeared in a school
play at Chadwick. I had to wear a monkey suit. Dad and
Nancy picked me up afterward. It was hot, and when
I sat down in the back of Dad's convertible, I got sick.
I threw up in the area behind the seat where the top was
stored, but I never said a word about it. He must have
had to put the top down at some point and discovered
the mess, although, to this day, he has never mentioned
it.
    That's just the kind of father he was. He never raised
his hand to us, and it took a lot to get him to raise
his voice. Whenever I did something wrong, he just
gave me that Ronald Reagan look, and I felt guilty. I always
listened to him, but I never told him my problems because
I thought that would be a sign of weakness and it might
be a reason for him not to like me.

—MICHAEL REAGAN *(son of*
former President RONALD REAGAN)

One night I was playing tag when I fell and split my head
open. I was bleeding and crying. The other kids picked
me up and were carrying me home. I looked up and
saw my father walking home on the other side of the
street. I was so glad to see Pa. He looked over at me, and
said, "That's what you get for going out and playing."
I would have given anything if he had come over to
me, leaned down, and said. "Son, how do you feel?
Are you all right?" But he wasn't capable of that.

Years later, I was told that my father went to see [my movie] *Champion* with one of his drinking buddies. When I was being slaughtered by my opponent in the ring, my father covered his face with both hands. At the end of the fight, when I was finally winning, Pa got up and yelled in broken English, "Issur, give it to him! Issur, give it to him!"

If only Pa could have said, "Issur, give it to him," when I was a kid. Pa covered his eyes when Kirk Douglas was bleeding makeup in a movie. But when Issur was being carried home, head bleeding for real, Pa was on the other side of the street, grumbling, "That's what you get for playing." He should have covered his eyes then. Years later, many people told me how Pa would brag about me. But it was too late to get that pat on the back when Pa was dead.

—KIRK DOUGLAS

When I was a boy my father's silence was one of the great mysteries of my life. Not only did he fail to answer when I spoke to him, he didn't even seem to hear me. There was no sign, no flicker in his face, to show that I had spoken, and I sometimes wondered whether I actually had. I used to stand there and listen, trying to catch the echo of my voice.

—ANATOLE BROYARD, 1920–1990
(former editor of the
New York Times
Sunday book review section)

When I started to play in organized games, I could go four for four, and he'd get all over me for some fielding lapse. To friends and neighbors, he'd always be building me up, but it was sure tough to drag a compliment out of him directly. He even had a similar relationship with my mom, Ruth. When Dad was around, everyone in the house, including Mom, was intimidated. It seemed as

though her chief responsibility was to keep us out of
trouble so that Dad wouldn't get mad at us.

—THURMAN MUNSON
(New York Yankees catcher)

My father, Jim Russo, was a World War II veteran who'd
been on the beach at D day and made it all the way to
Berlin. I, on the other hand, grew up during Vietnam
and protested against it. Though we didn't have the
kinds of fights that a lot of WWII fathers had with their
sons, it was later, in the 1980s, after there was a decade
between us and any disagreement we might have had,
before he told me his war experiences. One afternoon
he just started talking, telling me things I know he hadn't
told my mother or anybody since coming back. Some of
it was very grisly. Some of it was very funny. Some
of it was very grisly and very funny. But they were
clearly things he hadn't talked about in a long time. I was
awfully glad to be around that day. I was finally old enough
to not be blasé and superior as I would have been when
I was an eighteen-year-old war protestor.

   Not too long after, my father died of cancer. It's a terrible
thing, but when you know death is coming, you contemplate
what is going to happen. There weren't an awful lot
of things I wanted to say to him that didn't get said,
which is not to say there was an awful lot said. The most
highly verbal things I had to say I've said in my fiction.
The Risk Pool is about a father and son who manage
to communicate but don't actually talk to each other.
It is about how men communicate with each other through
third parties.

   We weren't effusive about our feelings. He wasn't
that kind of man and I suppose neither am I. But I don't
worry about things left unspoken. There was a lot of just
being in the same neighborhood that was really grand.

—RICHARD RUSSO *(novelist)*

Absence

For much of my life, I had no image of my father. He left us when I was only a year old, and until I saw him again when I was nine, I had no real idea of who he was, what type of person he was, nothing. I only knew that he was living with another woman in Southern California, a woman he would eventually marry. That alone was enough to make me hate him. I hated the fact that he left my mother alone to fend for herself. In those few years before I saw him again, I came to think of him only as an evil man because only an evil man would leave his wife and son.

. . . Thoughts of my father bugged me throughout my life. When I was young, I would see other kids with their fathers and felt empty, like I was being cheated. I missed his companionship. I missed having an older friend. For a while when I was still young, I talked to him quite a bit, even though it wasn't easy. He would call from California, and I was excited to talk to him. As long as I was talking to him I was content. On the phone he was my father. He was what he was supposed to be. But as soon as we hung up, it was like everything went quiet, like I was suddenly alone. After a while, he didn't call very often. I didn't have anything to say to him anyway.

When I last saw [my uncle Simon], he told me that he wanted me to be at peace, and he knew that wouldn't happen until I started to form some kind of relationship with my father. My father had also confided in him that he was troubled by what he had done, that he was truly sorry but didn't know how he could make up for the past. Uncle Simon told me that it was time for me to start trying to forget the past because you never know what turns life takes. Two weeks later he died.

I always listened to Uncle Simon, but I didn't really need

him to tell me to seek out my father. It was something
I wanted to do for myself. I wanted to have a
relationship with my father. But neither one of us knew
where to start.

All I can say about my father now is that I'm cautious,
extremely cautious. You just can't not see someone for
more than ten years and pretend that nothing's
changed. It's impossible.

Now that I have my own child, my daughter, Christiana,
I realize even more the importance of a father's care
and love. I want Christiana to know her grandfather,
but I cannot get rid of the images and emotions in the
back of my mind. I can't forget that he left, and I can't
forget that he didn't communicate with his children,
his sons.

I'd like nothing more than for Frank and Charles Barkley
to someday be a true father and son. I'd like to rebuild
that trust. But only time can do that. He still lives in
Los Angeles and we talk on a regular basis. There's
no more pain. Bygones are bygones. I'm not holding a
grudge. A father is something I want, but I don't want
to jump into it wholeheartedly.

After all these years, I just can't. Not yet.

—CHARLES BARKLEY
(basketball player)

🍂

Remember "The Brady Bunch" from television? They were
the perfect family. Everybody loved them. I hated them.
I hated them because they had a mother and a father
and enough food on the table for all of them.

We never had enough food. But at least I could beat on
other kids and steal their lunch money and buy myself
something to eat. I could steal candy bars, too. But I
couldn't steal a father. I couldn't steal a father's
hug when I needed one. I couldn't steal a father's
ass-whipping when I needed one. I didn't have a man to
look up to, or to listen to.

Biologically, I did have a father, of course. His name
was—and is—A. D. Adams, and he used to work in the
steel mills, like most of the men in Bessemer [Alabama].

He was my father and the father of two of my sisters.
He was married, but not to my mother. He had his own
family on the other side of town. He'd come by
sometimes and give me a little money, but then I wouldn't
see him again for months.

—BO JACKSON
(football and baseball player)

My father's dying when I was very young created the
obvious problems we all read about when we first learn
to spell psychology. I first invented him using little more
than a handful of memories so fragmented they were
like strobe light freeze-frames in the theater.

Later I began casting about for surrogates. As I settled
into journalism I took my father figures from the older
men along the way—editors, executives, always
authority figures, never reporters; reporters are footloose,
irresponsible corsairs according to the newspaper myth
of my youth. One wanted to be a reporter. They were
the romantic devils. But one would not have wanted
a reporter for a father. So I tended toward bosses.

Rather late in the day, I realized that I had been a somewhat
inferior father. Looking back on events, I realized that
I had never been much interested in being a father. Of
course I loved the children, but nowadays I see fathers whose
lives are to some extent devoted to careers in fatherhood.
They study the role, live it as a role, and take pride in
doing it well, suffer when they do it inadequately.

It never occurred to me to take fatherhood so seriously.
Though I had children, I remained a son while my children
were growing up. Offhand I don't know when I finally
quit searching for a father. But I did, and I slowly and
quietly realized that I had turned into the father figures
I'd spent my life seeking, and that I wasn't cutting a very
good one for my children. I am still not very good at
it. The role doesn't come naturally to me. I feel like
an impostor, and I laugh privately at myself faking it. Being
eternal son was better.

—RUSSELL BAKER
*(*New York Times *humor columnist)*

With my father, there wasn't a lot of communication.
My father . . . was not very successful at living life. I loved
him, you know? But there's people that lack an ability to
live life. I mean, life just pummels them, and they die.
A lot of people, they just get hit—hit! hit! hit!—hit so
much their perspective on life is so altered that they can't
even come up for air. I believe this: When people do things
that are mean, or, even unintentionally, that aren't good
towards life and people—they're the ones that suffer
more than anybody else. If they're a good person, they
will really eat themselves alive. And I think that's what
happened to him. He had a very unhappy life, got
cancer, and . . . my heart went out to him. . . . I didn't
see him for about ten years. I didn't know anything about
him.

—Tom Cruise
(actor, son of an electrical engineer
who divorced Cruise's mother
when he was eleven)

My father died in 1960. He was an intellectual. . . . She
[my mother] made the money and he read a lot. He wasn't
successful or ambitious. He spoke lots of languages.
There were times that kids said to me, what does your
father do? and I had to make something up because I actually
didn't know what he did.

—David Geffen *(entertainment mogul)*

My dad never communicated easily. Oh, he got his various
points across, mostly through intimidation and fear. I don't
remember him ever giving me a hug or a kiss. Things
were done his way, no argument otherwise. Every two
years or so he decided to paint the outside of the house,
which meant that I was dragged into the drudgery as his
assistant. It was like doing jail time.
   Once he was mixing paint and drinking coffee. I tried
cracking a joke. My dad responded by glaring up at me

and saying, "How would you like a cup of coffee in your
face?" . . . The next time we painted—the interior, this
time—he kicked a bucket of green paint over, spilling
it on the carpet. I was so delighted I had to take a break
and leave the room.

But I also wanted desperately to please him. Shortly after
settling into our new home, we got word that our car
was repaired. My dad and I took a train back to
Wyoming, where we picked up the car and started driving
it back. Somewhere in the desert, we picked up a sailor
who was hitching a ride. My dad told me to get into
the back seat.

After a while I noticed the door wasn't locked, which
I decided to correct. For some reason, though, instead of
pushing the handle down, I pulled it up. The car was
doing about seventy miles per hour. Because of the
speed at which we were traveling, the door blew open.
It happened so suddenly that I was still holding the handle,
and I was yanked outside.

I hit the road like a sack of potatoes and went rolling
over the gravel. The rocks punctured my body and cracked
my skull open. Inexplicably, I didn't lose consciousness.
And after I stopped rolling, I sprang up and started
limping back toward the car. My dad had been driving
so fast that it took him half a mile to stop, which made
me think he didn't know I had fallen out.

"Daddy! Daddy!" I yelled, "Wait for me!"

Then I saw him turn the car around and come back
toward me. I was relieved. The panic drained out of me.
When my father stepped out of the car, he looked as if
he'd seen a ghost. His face registered shock. I didn't
realize the extent of my injuries, so naturally I assumed
that I had done something bad and started apologizing.

"Please don't hit me, Daddy," I cried. "Please don't hit
me. I'm sorry. Really sorry."

Without saying a word, my dad scooped me up in
muscular arms and carried me back to the car. I saw the
bloodstains mottle his shirt, which is when I discovered
that I was hurt more than I had realized. My father,
showing more concern than I'd ever imagined he could,
slid into the back with me still cradled in his arms and
told the sailor to drive.

"Try to find a hospital," my dad instructed.

The sailor felt awful. He knew that if we hadn't picked him up, I wouldn't have fallen out. But he found a hospital. Admitted right away, I remember the doctors had trouble removing the gravel from my skin. It took a long time. When they finally sewed me up and bandaged me, I looked like a pint-size mummy, wrapped from head to toe. I even bled under each fingernail.

Thanks to the painkillers the docs gave me, the rest of the drive was a blur. When we pulled into our driveway, my dad checked me out, then told me to wait in the car for a minute. He wanted to explain to my mother what had happened before she saw me. Soften the blow a bit. My mom came running out of the house like a woman fleeing a fire, and headed straight for the car. By then, blood had soaked through my bandages, so when she glimpsed me, she went to pieces.

"My baby!" she howled. "What happened to my baby?"

My father got his chance to explain the entire incident. My mom went to pieces, though by the time she'd heard the tale, cooler heads prevailed. She watched my father carry me inside and put me to bed. They stood over me for a while. Thinking I was asleep, my mother asked my dad to repeat the story, and as he did, he began to cry.

"My boy," my dad sobbed, "he stood on the road and said to his papa, 'Don't hit me, Daddy, please don't hit me.' "

It was so difficult for him to say I love you, and right then he was paying the price for it. Years later, I made my share of mistakes as a father. But saying I love you wasn't one of them. Though he never said the words, I'm sure my dad believed his kids knew that he loved them. Anyway, that night he cried for a long time.

—SONNY BONO
(musician and politician)

🍃

There isn't a whole lot I can recall about the time my mother and father were together, what with his five-days-on, five-

days-off schedule, and their complete breakup by the
time I was three. But I do remember hearing voices raised
in the front room a few times while [my brother] Steve
and I were in bed, knowing it was some kind of argument,
wondering what would happen next. There were never any
fisticuffs, never anything like that. And there were good
times, too. But much of the time they spent together
they were at each other. Nothing a three-year-old could
understand, though later, growing up with my mother, I
would hear her version of it, which was that my father
wasn't very interested in fatherhood or responsibility,
and after he left he often didn't come through with the
child support the court had ordered.

  Now, I realize, it wasn't as simple as that, and on
those rare occasions I see my father he'll sometimes
offer his version, about how energetic he was, how he was
always looking for ways to make money, about the plans
he had for us, about the time he wanted to invest in
some old houses, fix them up and sell them, but my
mother nixed the deal. In any event, they just didn't see
eye to eye, as he puts it. And then he was gone.

—DAVE WINFIELD *(baseball slugger)*

I remember thinking when they first told me he had died,
if he had only dropped by once to say hello. Surely, he
must have seen me on TV. Everybody else in the
country did. I never was angry about Pop leaving us.
I figured there must be something between him and Mom
that I didn't know about. He always was okay with me.
He had a great sense of humor, that I do remember.
If he had just dropped by once. Just once.

—JACKIE GLEASON, 1916-1987
(actor and comedian)

My father wasn't there like most fathers, but, in a way,
that can be a blessing. Familiarity breeds contempt, right?

—JACK FORD *(son of former
President* GERALD FORD)

I was two years old when [my father] came home. Mother said "Do you want to see him?" He said "No, I'll wait till morning." He'd been in Aden or somewhere [on military service], and he came home after two years, after not seeing me born or anything.

—ELTON JOHN *(singer)*

III
QUESTIONS

What Happened to His Dreams?

He had lost a son before I was born who died at age six of a burst appendix. Then they had me and my little brother. I was like his fair-haired boy. He took me everywhere because he had lost a son. He took me to baseball games. He owned a bar and grill and I used to sit up on the bar. He was very attentive to me and he knew all the cops. I had my own little police uniform when I was three years old. I had a badge with my name on it, official New York City police badge. The day he died, it was a cop who told me. A cop took me for a ride in a squad car. They didn't know how to tell my mother.

He was from Russia and he loved America and he tried to enlist in WWII and they wouldn't take him. So he sold his bar and went to work in a defense plant, building ships in Kearny, NJ, and he worked the overnight shift, and one night on the bus, he just keeled over and died. They came to tell us the next morning. I was coming home from the library. I remember hearing my mother crying and a cop ran down the stairs and grabbed me, picked me up and put me in the squad car and we drove around and he told me. It changed my life. I went from being a good student to a poor student. I didn't go to his funeral. I must have been angry. I think I was mad at him for leaving me, that's my only guess.

—LARRY KING

I can remember being awakened some mornings by the sound of talking downstairs, and, tiptoeing down the steps, I would find my father in motion, deep in conversation

with himself, dressed in a robe haphazardly tied, a cigar
stuck in the corner of his mouth, head cocked to one side,
ashes tumbling onto the burgundy robe as he paced the
room.

   What were his aspirations? I've often wondered since.
What are his regrets? He is a man who wanted more than
anything else to participate in the events of his day, who
came to Washington to be a participant and, by the age
of forty, found himself excluded.

—CARL BERNSTEIN
(*journalist*)

🍃

He (my father, photographed in his soldier's uniform after
the end of WWII) looked like John Garfield in this great
suit, he looked like he was going to eat the
photographer's head off. I couldn't ever remember him
looking that defiant or proud when I was growing up. I
used to wonder what happened to all that pride, how it
turned into so much bitterness.

—BRUCE SPRINGSTEEN

🍃

My dad probably would have had the drive to be a pro
if he had had the inclination. I mean, he was the world's
original hard-nosed competitor. I'm sure that's where
I inherited my desire from. Dad would think nothing
of hitting us ground balls for hours, and if one took a bad
hop and bloodied a nose, he'd just go right on hitting without
stopping.

—THURMAN MUNSON

🍃

At the risk of never knowing certain things about my
father, I chose to spare him questions that would indicate
my doubt that he would survive his bout with cancer.
I wondered about his dreams. I'm not really sure if I
know what they were. I would like to have known how
he thought his life could've been better.

He worked for nearly thirty-seven years driving a *Daily News* truck, a job he said he "loved." Whether he loved it or not, he did it without complaint. This was something I was puzzled by.

As I was graduating from high school so did he (returning for his diploma at night), and then both of us went to the same college as freshmen at the same time. Pretty strange indeed! I left after one semester and he continued for three years, working his job at night and going to school in the day.

Shortly before he died, I found out it had been my father's ambition to become a comedian like his older brother, Pully, who was in thirty movies, starred in *Guys and Dolls,* and was a legendary nightclub performer. Pully had discouraged him from life on the road and pushed him to return home to the Bronx and raise his family.

In the end my questions about his personal fulfillment seemed pretty trivial compared to the need to thank him for the sacrifices he made in being my father. But during his illness, which was painful and scary and, in a strange way, beautiful as well, I didn't do that either. I didn't want to mess with his determination as long as he had the will to live and the hope of recovery.

Unfortunately, I have come to understand that it was my fear and partial inability to deal with his death that kept me from talking about things.

—STEWART LERMAN *(record producer)*

I was the son of an actor . . . and I was with my dad in Hollywood in the early days, and I saw him sell out. . . . He didn't do stage any more. He kept hoping that the movie industry would do something, and he was in the middle of a change in the industry, and he went downhill, then became self-destructive and disintegrated before my eyes. And to have your best friend disintegrate . . .

—JASON ROBARDS, JR. *(actor)*

What Did He Really Think?

He was hospitalized when I was six. What I learned about him was mostly from other people. And these stories I continue to hear even today.

One of my favorites is about the time he was raising money for something, singing at a benefit, with Sonny Terry and Brownie McGhee, two well-known blues men who were both Black. They performed together and had a wonderful concert, and after the show, they ushered them into a nice dining room, and the maitre d' took Sonny Terry and Brownie McGhee and led them into the kitchen and said, "You folks will be eating in here of course."

When my dad found out that they weren't expected to eat with the other performers, he became amused, to say the least, and turned over all of the tables with all of the food in the restaurant. He said, "If it's good enough for us to sing together, it's got to be good enough for us to eat together. If it ain't good enough to eat together, no one's eating."

When Sonny Terry told me that story he had a flame in his eye.

—Arlo Guthrie

Six weeks after his death my father appeared to me in a dream. Suddenly he stood before me and said that he was coming back from his holiday. He had made a good recovery and was now coming home. I thought he would be annoyed with me for having moved into his room. But not a bit of it! Nevertheless, I felt ashamed because I had imagined he was dead. Two days later the dream was repeated. My father had recovered and was coming home, and again I reproached myself because I had thought he was dead. Later I kept asking myself: "What does it mean that my father returns in dreams and that he seems so real?" It was an unforgettable experience, and it forced me for the first time to think about life after death.

—C.G. JUNG, 1875–1961
(father of analytical psychology)

❧

Until I was thirteen years old, my father, who was born in 1875, did not make a great mark on my life. I adored him, but the two of us did not indulge in the usual forms of father-son camaraderie such as ball-playing, hunting, and fishing. My first impressions of him are of an older man dressed in rather somber clothing, either driving a pick-up truck, going to work as an accountant, or going to church. That, it seemed to me, is what he did mostly. . . . He faithfully went to church on Sunday mornings and evenings and to prayer meetings on Wednesday evenings. He often read the Bible between times. He said his prayers while kneeling at his bedside before he retired each evening and, on the rare occasions when my family dined alone (generally at Thanksgiving and Christmas), he said grace before meals. I once rode with him in his pick-up truck, and in a minor emergency when he slammed on the brakes to avoid hitting another car he said "damn." I was a bit terrified. He often used expressions of exasperation, "dadblameit," "dadgumnit," and "dadblastit." I'm certain it never entered his consciousness that dadgumnit was simply a substitution of syllables for goddamnit.

—CRAIG CLAIBORNE
*(longtime food editor
for the* New York Times)

❧

I keep wondering what Dad must be feeling, what he must be thinking, sitting there in his wheelchair. I hope he's

thinking: "I am the man whose two sons won more
big-league games than any brothers in baseball
history."

—PHIL NIEKRO
(pro baseball pitcher)

🌢

Papa is lying in bed watching me, his strange eyes staring
at me with a queer, uncanny wonder as if, in that veiled
borderland between Life and Death in which his soul
drifts suspended, a real living being of his own
flesh and blood were an incongruous and puzzling
spectacle. I feel as if my health, the suntan on
my face contrasted with the unhealthy pallor of his,
were a spiritual intrusion, an impudence. And yet how
his eyes lighted up with grateful affection when he first
saw me! It made me feel so glad, so happy I had
come! . . .
     He was asleep when I was writing the above. Then
he woke up and called me over. He made a dreadful effort
to speak clearly and I understood a part of what he said.
"Glad to go, boy—a better sort of life—another sort—
somewhere"—and then he mumbled. He appeared to
be trying to tell me what sort—and although I tried my
damnedest I couldn't understand! . . . Then he became
clear again: "this sort of life—froth!—rotten—all of
it—no good!" There was a bitter expression on his
poor, sunken face. And there you have it—the verdict
of a good man looking back over seventy-six years: "Froth!
Rotten!"

—EUGENE O'NEILL, 1888–1953
(dramatist, in a letter to his wife
at his father's deathbed)

🌢

My father always enjoyed a good laugh but not at himself.
Once I gave him Clarence Day's *Life with Father* to read.
I was a little afraid he would see a picture of himself
in it and resent it. But not at all. When I asked him

how he liked it, he slapped his knee and said, "By God, that's just like your grandfather."

—ROGER BALDWIN, 1884-1981
*(founder of the American
Civil Liberties Union)*

🍂

The relationship between a father who happened to be President and a son working on his staff was one problem that I never found serious. Between the two of us the situation was eased by our common military background. In person I always called him "Dad," and we spoke our minds to each other frankly. However, when speaking of him in the third person, I would use the common term "the Boss" and sometimes even slipped unconsciously into "the President. . . ."

The situation was easier, I believe, than it would have been if my father had been president of a corporation. At least in the White House, nobody was concerned that I would inherit the job. Therefore, I felt that I was treated as just another staff officer by my colleagues unless a tricky or unpleasant issue came up which someone would ask me to discuss with Dad at some "informal opportune time. . . ." The only problem in the long run was with the Boss himself. He was a man who in his later years (in contrast to those days of slave labor during the thirties) chose to leave his worries at the office. From the White House days to the end, I think he unconsciously associated me with work—and bad news at that!

—JOHN S.D. EISENHOWER

🍂

While he was in the hospital in his last few weeks, we kept a tape recorder or CD player playing because he liked to listen to music. He'd float in and out of consciousness, so the common thread was music. He'd react to the music a bit, sort of move his hands as if he were keeping time. Basically we played the music of his friends and contemporaries: Ellington, Basie, Nat Cole, Tony Bennett. Two nights before he passed away, the

Ellington record that had been playing ended, and sort
of rhetorically we asked what he'd like to hear. He hadn't
spoken in four weeks, and suddenly and forcibly he spoke
his last words: "Basie." We were like the Keystone Cops
falling all over ourselves to put the Count on the box.
Basie was his friend for fifty years and Dad was obviously
really hurt when he passed. My dad always used to say
if he was going to heaven he wasn't going to get there
until they had a great band, and nearly everybody of
his generation is there now, with the exception of Max
Roach and a few others. My sisters and I say Basie must
have sent a note down to him saying something like,
"All right man, let's go, tour starts Wednesday night!"

—ED ECKSTINE

"**N**o," Dad said to me, "the Christian ministry isn't a
job you choose, it's a vocation for which you got to receive
a call." I could tell he wanted me to ask him. We never
talked much, but we understood each other, we were
both scared devils, not like you and the kid. I asked him.
Had he ever received the call? He said No. He said No,
he never had. Received the call. That was a terrible
thing for him to admit. And I was the one he told. As
far as I knew he never admitted it to anybody, but he admitted
it to me. He felt like hell about it, I could tell. That was
all we ever said about it. That was enough.

—JOHN UPDIKE *(writer)*

October. *Here in this dank, unfamiliar kitchen*
I study my father's embarrassed young man's face.
Sheepish grin, he holds in one hand a string
Of spiny yellow perch, in the other
A bottle of Carlsbad beer.

In jeans and denim shirt, he leans
Against the front fender of a Ford circa 1934.
He would like to pose bluff

and hearty for his posterity,
Wear his old hat cocked over his ear,
stick out his tongue . . .
All his life my father wanted to be bold.

But the eyes gave him away, and the hands
That limply offer a string of dead perch
And the bottle of beer. Father, I loved you,
Yet how can I say thank you,
I who cannot hold my liquor either
And do not even know the places to fish?
                                   —RAYMOND CARVER, 1938-1988
                                                   (writer)

Always a man of habit, he would leave for work early
in the morning, work hard all day, and then, when he came
home (on those days he did not work late), take a short
nap before dinner. Sometime during our first week in
the new house, before we had properly moved in, he made
a curious kind of mistake. Instead of driving home to the
new house after work, he went directly to the old one,
as he had done for years, parked his car in the
driveway, walked into the house through the back door,
climbed the stairs, entered the bedroom, lay down on the
bed, and went to sleep. He slept for about an hour.
Needless to say, when the new mistress of the house
returned to find a strange man sleeping in her bed, she
was a little surprised. But unlike Goldilocks, my father did
not jump up and run away. The confusion was eventually
settled, and everyone had a good laugh. Even today,
it still makes me laugh. And yet, for all that, I cannot help
regarding it as a pathetic story. It is one thing for a man
to drive to his old house by mistake, but it is quite
another, I think, for him not to notice that anything
has changed inside it. Even the most tired or distracted
mind has a corner of pure, animal response, and can give
the body a sense of where it is. One would have to be
nearly unconscious not to see, or at least not to feel,
that the house was no longer the same. "Habit," as one
of Beckett's characters says, "is a great deadener."

And if the mind is unable to respond to the physical evidence, what will it do when confronted with the emotional evidence?

—PAUL AUSTER *(novelist)*

IV
LOVE

Things I'm Glad I Said to My Father

One night in January, he presented me with one of [his] notebooks. He asked if I would mind looking at it.

We were in the dining room. I sat in a chair and read from the journal he had given me. He sat in another chair and watched. He asked what I thought. I said I thought that the journal was interesting; I thought it beautifully written. He asked me to read some more. I did read some more. At one point I looked up, and I could see that he was crying. He was not sobbing, but tears were running down his cheeks. I didn't say anything. I went back to reading. When I looked up again, he seemed composed.

I told him I liked it.

—BENJAMIN CHEEVER
(son of writer JOHN CHEEVER)

My dad would have liked me to become a lawyer, like he was, and have a real profession. One afternoon, during college, he was in Toronto on business and we had lunch. I said, "Dad, I have to take a year off from academia and try music as a career. Here's the deal: If at the end of the year, I'm not making a living, I'll go back to school. Maybe law school. I don't know."

He said, "I was kind of expecting this." But he gave me his blessing. I had a year to make it.

—PAUL SHAFFER *(musician)*

One time I played out here in Los Angeles, and every time you play at home it makes you kind of nervous, because it's home and you know people, everyone hates it. After the show, my father was the first person back, and instead of saying something like, "Nice work, sonny," he said, "What's the matter, you got a cold?"

I should have said something there. It's actually sort of awful.

Later, he was sick by this time, I got nominated for an Academy Award for the song from *Parenthood*. I long ago had given up talking about what was going on with me and my work because I knew I'd get slammed. But I forgot this time. He was lying in bed watching television, which is how we had our conversations. It was like the television was our psychiatrist. We never looked at each other. We'd both look at the television. I'd lie on the bed next to him or otherwise I'd have to be standing up.

I knew it was a mistake, but I said, "I got nominated for an Academy Award today, Dad."

He said, "For what?"

"For a song from *Parenthood*, 'Love to Hear Your Smile,' " I said.

"Never heard of it," he said.

So I said, "Well of course you never heard of it, you're lying here watching television all the time."

And he said, "Well I never saw it on television."

So then I finally said to him. "Why couldn't you just say, 'nice work boy?' "

"Well I'm just telling the truth," was his answer.

—RANDY NEWMAN

✿

He'd take me out and get to drinking. We'd go to a joint called the Jackson Bar. He'd sit me up on the stool and start throwing back V.O. like it was water. Get all loud and rowdy and ready to destroy Detroit. Funny, he liked to fight his friends.

"Daddy," I'd say, "we better go."

And that'd be it. He'd chill, just 'cause I told him to.

—SMOKEY ROBINSON *(singer)*

I used to fight back all the time. My father was one tough
son-of-a-gun. My father respects me because I stood up
to him.

—DONALD TRUMP

~

You hear a lot about unconditional love. I don't think
I was aware, growing up, of how rare and special it is.
But I definitely feel that I received it. . . . With my dad
I feel a sense of continuity, like we're in the same race,
and he's passing on the baton. Talking about it sounds
corny, but if I were sitting alone with my dad, it wouldn't
be unusual for me to talk about how much I love him.
  I know he'd say the same thing about me. It's almost
like we're the same person.

—JEFF BRIDGES
(actor, son of LLOYD BRIDGES)

~

My parents and I came to this country from Cuba when
I was five in an effort to improve our lives and gain freedom
to do things we weren't allowed to do there. With that
in mind it gives you a perspective of unity, hard work,
perseverance, confidence, and faith, because you really
started out with nothing. With Latin people, family unity
means a lot. That is our legacy, we place a lot of value
on our heritage. I still live at home and our
communication has gotten better in the last few years. I
tell my father about all the ways he has helped me and
how much I love him. I do that on a daily or weekly
basis. I try to never let what he does for me go
unnoticed.

—JON SECADA

~

He was easy to locate. I had only to ask an operator for
his telephone number and address. Yet it took me years.
  I picked up the receiver, reviewed in my mind what

I wanted to say and dialed the number. A young woman answered.

"I'm looking for a Bernard J. Goldman," I said. "Is he there?"

"Yes, just a minute."

"Hello." It was a man's voice this time, strong and clear.

I hesitated. My chest was moving toward my backbone and I had trouble drawing breath.

"My name is Michael Norman, but it used to Michael Goldman, and I'm looking for my father."

He hesitated. ". . . ah . . . I had a son named Michael Goldman . . . ah . . . he would be about thirty-five or thirty-six, something like that?"

"He's thirty-two," I said. "I think you're my father."

I waited for the voice to come back. I had prepared myself for nothing beyond this point. I could feel the pulse in my palm.

"Well, if you're my son, I'm very pleased to hear from you."

"How are you?" I asked, fumbling for something less banal to say after more than two decades of silence.

"I'm fine," he said. "Where are you calling from?"

. . . I was afraid, of course, afraid that one of us would disappoint the other. The child in the man wanted badly to please the father and wanted the father to please him. But I also knew that this first meeting with my father could be the last. He had walked away twenty-one years ago and could easily do it again—and I was no longer a well-armored boy. I had loosened my breastplate. I was exposed.

He was short, maybe five feet six, noticeably shorter than I. His hands were small. And as he came toward me, he moved with a slight limp.

"Dad?" I said, still not sure, and put out my hand to greet him. He seized it and in an instant pulled me to him and embraced me. "Michael," he said. "It's been so long, Michael . . . Michael."

I stiffened. I could not bring myself to return the affection of this man I still considered a stranger. I could not in one moment, as my father was doing so well, close the distance that two decades had put between us. Still, I did not want to push him away now that we had finally come together.

The gap had narrowed, and in time I hoped it would close. It was enough for now to accept the idea of having a father, an idea I had rejected as a child and resisted as a man.

—MICHAEL NORMAN
(New York Times *correspondent*)

Enduring Love

I think of my father every day. My mother too. It comes
up in some way. There'll be a fight on and I'll think he
might not know about this, he'd like to watch it, and
I think about calling. Sometimes I think all this terrible,
competitive stuff, all the bragging he used to do about being
the strongest, and the smartest and the fastest was the
main thing. But in a lot of ways the main thing was
his sense of humor. I think I've been a better father.
And that would be one of the most important things to
me. If you want something written on your tombstone,
that wouldn't be so bad. That you did a little better
as a father than the last one.

—RANDY NEWMAN

On May 30, 1960, my father died of cancer at age eighty-six
in Santa Cruz, California. . . . He was not only good but
also kind, wise, and cheerful. He had no fear of death.
He never thought of life as anything but a hard passage
to a heavenly rest. He believed with the utmost confidence,
as did my mother, that we would all meet again on the
other side. I was at his bedside when he regained
consciousness after a four-and-a-half-hour operation.
"Where are we, Jimmy?" he said. "Are we in heaven?"
I was never able to achieve his redemptive faith, though
I tried, but he has lived every day in my memory. I wake
sometimes in the night, hearing his voice, or when
walking alone, suddenly I think I see him at my side.

—JAMES RESTON
*(Pulitzer Prize-winning
Washington correspondent
for the* New York Times)

My father had given me so much, in so many ways, and now I wanted to give something to him. How about the 100-meter medal from '84? [one of six Olympic gold medals he won in track and field]. It is the one thing I could give him to represent all the good things we did together, all the positive things that happened to me because of him.

I had never before taken any of my medals out of the bank vault where I kept them. But that day, on the way to the airport, I stopped at the bank to get the medal, and I put it in the pocket of my suit jacket. I would take it to New Jersey—for Dad. . . .

The day of the funeral, when our family was viewing the body, I pulled out the medal to place in my father's hand. . . . My mother asked me if I was sure I wanted to bury the medal, and I was. It would be my father's forever. "But I'm going to get another one," I told my mother. Turning to my father, I said, "Don't worry. I'm going to get another one." That was a promise—to myself and to Dad. He was lying there so peacefully, his hands resting on his chest. When I placed the medal in his hand, it fit perfectly.

—CARL LEWIS
(track and field champion)

He has just been buried. I shall never forget these terrible three days; the hideous suspense of the ride on; the dull inert sorrow, during which I felt as if I had been stunned, or as if part of my life had been taken away, and the two moments of sharp, bitter agony, when I kissed the dear, dead face and realized that he would never again on this earth speak to me or greet me with his loving smile, and then when I heard the sound of the first clod dropping on the coffin holding the one I loved dearest on earth . . . I feel that if it were not for the certainty that, as he himself has so often said, "he is not dead but gone before," I should almost perish. With the help of my God I will try to lead such a life as he would have wished.

—THEODORE ROOSEVELT, 1858-1919
(in his personal diary)

Sometimes I forget that you have gone
You've gone and you're not coming back.
And it's hard to believe you're still not here
What's left behind disputes that fact.
Your closet's still full of your clothes and your shoes
And your bookcase still holds all your books
It's as if all you'd done was to go out of town
You'll be back soon that's just how it looks.
But your suitcase is empty it's right here in the hall
And that's not even the strangest thing
Why would you leave your wallet behind?
Your glasses, your wristwatch, and ring?

Sometimes I forget that you have gone
And that we'll never see you again.
I think for a moment "I gotta give him a call."
But I can't now I realize then.
No, we can't meet for lunch at the usual place.
At the place where we always would go.
And there was something I wanted to tell you so bad
Something I knew that you'd want to know.
I could go by myself to our old haunt
But that seems such a strange thing to do.
The waiters would wonder what was going on.
Why weren't you there, where were you?

Sometimes I forget that you have gone
I remember and I feel the ache.
How could it have happened? How could it be?
It's not true, there must be some mistake.
Momentos and memories tell me what good are they?
No, they're not much to have and to hold.
And it's true that you've gone and you're not coming back
And this world seems so empty and cold.
But sometimes something happens and it doesn't
    seem strange
You're not far away, you're near
Sometimes I forget that you have gone

Sometimes it feels like you're right here.
Right now, it feels like you're right here.

—LOUDON WAINWRIGHT III
(singer and songwriter,
son of LOUDON WAINWRIGHT, JR.
Lyrics from "Sometimes I Forget")

Looking back, I suppose that one of the problems I had
about fatherhood was that I attached a kind of divinity
to the role. Not that I considered myself all-knowing.
But I did have this notion that a really good father
would have the answers to just about everything and the
power to make all things work out. I think it's likely that
my own father, who died a relatively young man,
suffered from the same sort of delusion. Even when
he seemed most confident and implacable, I would bet that
he was full of doubt, that his controlling family style was
a cover-up for the fear that he didn't really have much
power at all.

—LOUDON WAINWRIGHT, JR.
(editor at Life *magazine and*
father of LOUDON WAINWRIGHT III*)*

My father was in the hospital for fifteen years but you
could still understand him and he obviously understood
us. He was interested in what was going on in our
lives, in the everyday things. I didn't feel any
extraordinary need to talk philosophically while he was
sick. We didn't talk about rocket scientist stuff. We talked
about everyday things. The things that were exciting
in those days were that people around the world were
recording his songs. We brought him home from the
hospital on the weekends or went to visit him and we'd
bring the newest, latest, greatest records of people
recording his songs. That was a nice thing to share.
I also had started playing the guitar a little bit. He showed
me a few things on the guitar. We'd sit around the backyard

just playing music. There wasn't a whole lot that was
left unsaid for a kid.

—Arlo Guthrie

One of my earliest memories is of the first day I entered
school at the age of six when I went very proudly into Pop's
saloon and told him that I had learned a song. He gave
me a glass of sarsaparilla, set me up on the bar, and
told me to go ahead, whereupon I belted out this minor
classic:

> *Fly away, fly away, birdee-o, dadadada.*
> *Bring her a feather and bring her a song—*
> *And that will please birdee-o all the day long.*

We were a musical family, the piano always on the go,
and all of us invariably fooling around with a tune. I used
to sing, "I Want a Girl—Just Like the Girl Who Married
Dear Old Dad" for my mother and father, and they'd
sit there, holding hands, beaming like the summer sun.

Pop's gentle waywardness was thoroughly engrained.
He had the charm of an Irish minstrel, he did everything
to the tune of laughter—but he was totally deficient
in a sense of responsibility to his family. Despite this, he
always thought he was doing well for us. At times, things
got very rough. At best he had a spotty job record: here
a job, there a job, and long stretches of nothing in
between. This coincided with the Cagney boys all trying
to get through college and working after school, so that
at times it was only our part-time jobs that put the
groceries on the table . . .

But he was irrepressible. He sailed happily through life,
charming everyone, and all the time belting down the sauce
that I suppose helped to sustain both his charm and
his improvidence. When the flu epidemic of 1918 came
along, the inroads of all that booze made him an easy victim.
Dead in two swift, terrible days. My mother loved him deeply,
and his going was an agony for her. But despite the
terrible loss she felt after Pop left, despite the aching
sorrow she knew seeing her man die before her eyes, she

was staunch stuff. This sturdy lady kept the family intact, and we boys worked to help keep us all together.

—JAMES CAGNEY, 1899–1986 *(actor)*

Father had loved me more than his other children, perhaps because I was his only son, or because he saw in me the fulfillment of his own dream of becoming an engineer. I had been absolutely devoted to him. I remembered our frequent walks together, sometimes in silence, sometimes with him telling me about his new ideas. For me, these walks had been a gift; I recalled listening impatiently for the sound of the car door slamming shut, for that meant he was home from work. As we walked, I would tell him about my affairs, about new projects at our design bureau, and he would listen with great interest. Beginning when I was a child, he had taken me hunting—ducks in the winter and rabbits in summer. Our work on his memoirs, just he and I, had brought us even closer. . . .

He was not a cruel person. He was warm, very kind. He was a common person. He loved his family. He liked to do everything as a family.

—SERGEI KHRUSHCHEV
(son of NIKITA KHRUSHCHEV,
former leader of the Soviet Union)

Twenty stones in I saw the name William and wondered if they hadn't made a mistake. Then I kicked away some snow and saw the entire name:

LOUIE WILLIAM ANDERSON
BORN AUGUST 12, 1901–DIED APRIL 9, 1980
WORLD WAR I. BUGLER

From my little sack, I removed the black corduroy cap you wore, the one I remember you in, and placed it on the edge of the gravestone. I plugged the other set of the headphones I'd brought into the tape machine and

draped them on each side of the headstone. Earlier, I had
read each of these letters [from your family] into a tape
recorder. I wanted you to hear them and turned on the
tape player. I felt we should listen to them together.

With my voice reciting in the background, I removed
the glasses you wore, noticing how worn and well used
they were and how large your head must've been. They
slipped onto my head easily. How many times I
remember those glasses sitting on the edge of your
nose, your middle finger on the right hand pushing them
up so you could read your Webster's. Your eyes weren't
so bad. Looking through them, I could see pretty clearly.

Looking through your eyes, the world didn't seem
that bad. What did you see, I wondered, that I didn't?

I knew the answer. After all this, I knew

It wasn't the same with me, I realized. Even through
your eyes, I saw the world as a brighter, happier place.
And I was happy for that.

I . . . reached into my pocket and pulled out a white
envelope Mom had given me. It was filled with pictures
of us and a note from her that said, "Dear Louie, I hope
that these are okay. I hope the trip was a good one. Love,
Mother."

The first photo was of you and Mom, taken a long,
long time ago, probably when you still called her "my
darling Toy." In the next you two are sitting in a booth
at a restaurant. You have on a tuxedo and look handsome.
Was this before a performance? Another photo shows
all of us in South Dakota. I'm standing next to you.
I must've been about five years old. You have a cigarette
in one hand, your glasses—the ones I was wearing—are
on, and I have a baseball cap on, just as I do now.

Right now the tape is continuing on about your career,
but there're more pictures to sort through. Here's one of
you clowning around. Tears are starting to form in my
eyes. I can't help it anymore. I'm crying, I'm writing,
I'm looking at photographs. In this next picture, you're
older and sicker, holding a can of beer and smiling. The
tape continues to play but I can't hear it, and finally it
stops. The letters are over and now it's just you and
me, sitting out here in the blizzard.

Here's a photo of you rolling a Bull Durham. God, I can

almost smell the tobacco. You're smiling in the picture, and I know right now, at this moment, you're here with me. I'm crying hard and loud. I'm not holding anything back. I realize how much I miss you, you bastard. This last picture is a close-up of you. There is a cigarette in your mouth, and you're wearing the same hat and glasses that I have on now. I see the look on your face, in your eyes, and you're looking directly at me, and I hear you say, "I love you, Louie."

I know, Dad.

I forgive you. I understand.

I realize why I have come here and what I've been looking for all this time. I wanted to be with you. And now I am and always will be.

Oh yeah. There's one more thing that I haven't said but want to. And that one thing is, I love you.

—LOUIE ANDERSON *(comic)*

There are those who say they never really knew their father very well, and to them I say I am truly sorry.

—OSGOOD PERKINS
(eldest son of actor
ANTHONY PERKINS, *who died in 1992)*

The summer of 1933 was a welter of colliding emotions. On June 19 my father died. I came back from New York by train. As I rode from the station I was aware that flags were at half mast. My mother, in black, stood in the driveway next to a magnificently flowering rosebush covered in scarlet blooms. Some images cannot be erased.

My father was laid out on a chaise lounge in the upstairs sitting room—the old day nursery. It was his particular place. They'd dressed him in his dark blue velvet smoking jacket. Sunlight streamed into the room from the open French doors, and I sat down on a straight chair beside him. We were alone. I felt numb, wondering what I should be feeling. At some point I put out my hand and gently stroked his hair as I'd seen my mother do at the

end of a bad day. It felt like corn silk, and the scalp
beneath it was cool. After a bit I left, closing the door
carefully behind me so as not to disturb him. I went
through the empty house, down the veranda steps and
out into the back garden. I walked around the lily pool.
There was that goddamn legend carved into its cement
lip:

> *The kiss of the sun for pardon,*
> *The song of the birds for mirth—*

I don't think I read beyond that point. My father was
dead and I could not cry. Not yet. For him, "the passing
of time" had ended; and for me, the lighthouse beam
which he so hated [?] had gone dark.

—HUME CRONYN

We always had a tight relationship. We never went without.
He made sure we had everything we could. Growing up
in the projects, that was a lot.
  For all the wrong things he did in his life, I have no
regrets. He lived it the way he saw it but he kept my head
on straight. I'll remember the good things. He was my man.
He was my friend. No one can say he wasn't a father
to me or say he wasn't a man with principles and
dignity.

—TYRONE BOGUES
(NBA star. From the time he was twelve until he was twenty-
three, his father was in prison for armed robbery.)

The other night I had a dream in which my father slipped,
fell down the stairs, and hurt himself. As he started to get
up I said to him, "You always try to be so large and
tough, even when you are hurt, and you never let
anybody hold you." He turned to me, curled up in my arms,
and allowed me to hold him.

—SAM KEEN
(men's movement writer)

I was just back from a radio show at WGY in Schenectady when Andrew called to say, "Pop, I have bad news—Grandpa passed away."

We all knew it would happen at any time, but it's still not easy. I can't relate to it: I'm afraid to try, to feel the guilt of all that I did and all that I failed to do. I know the only right response is to love more deeply—more intelligently. I wonder how long it will take me to forget how good he was. I hope I don't live that long. . . .

Poppa and Momma are beautiful. They taught us so much. It's difficult to be reluctant to go forward with any worthwhile effort after thinking about how courageous they were. We have to remember.

—MARIO CUOMO
(governor of New York)

🌿

My dad was my best friend. We would go over to the lake and my dad would say, "I've got a little extra training for you to do." Then he would have me swim across the lake while he sat in the boat with the motor going, drinking a beer and cheering me on. Of course I'd dive right in, because I'd do anything my dad told me to.

At the Olympics I saw my dad in the grandstands, taking photos as I passed by in the procession. I looked over and he had the biggest smile. I think he was having the thrill of his life.

A few hours later [after I was informed of his death], I went into the shower, and that's when it hit me. I just couldn't understand why this had happened to me. I was crying and really struggling. I couldn't quite understand the timing of the whole situation—why after eighteen years of swimming, six days before the biggest event in my life, this was happening to me.

I walked out [six days later, to swim in the Olympic finals] and could feel the adrenaline rush—10,000 fans cheering. I was thinking of him, and in the back of my mind I could hear him cheering for me. That gave me a lift. I thought for sure I was going to be on fire.

After the race I was very disappointed in my performance

and I felt as though I let not only myself down but a
lot of others, because I was expected to win the gold
or at least be in the race for the medals. But basically it
was the spirit of my father, as well as the strength of my
mother, that enabled me to want to compete, and I felt
as though if I were to pull out that wasn't what my
father would have wanted me to do.

—RON KARNAUGH
*(Olympic swimmer, whose father
suffered a fatal heart attack
during the opening ceremonies
of the 1992 games)*

I didn't go to my father's funeral, but I heard my mother
and grandmother say there was no money for a headstone.
His grave was unmarked except for a cheap brass plate.
I went and asked the teacher who ran the workshop
if I could make a headstone for my father's grave. He let
me make a cross with a big heart-shaped wooden plaque.
Then he helped me with the lettering:

FRANK QUINN
BORN—1897
DIED—1926
IN LOVE
HIS SON, TONY

I went out to the cemetery one Saturday and planted
it in the grass in place of the brass plate.

—ANTHONY QUINN

My father went out every day with his horse and wagon,
from street to street yelling, "Rags! Any rags!" He would
usually be back by early afternoon. He never worked
a full day. Many times, as I was walking home from
school, I'd see him riding along on his wagon filled with
junk and rags. I'd race ahead, jump up on the back of the
wagon, and climb over the junk to sit alongside him.

I remember once thinking that this embarrassed him,
but I wanted so much to let him know that I wasn't
ashamed of him. I wanted so much to let him know how
much I loved him.

—KIRK DOUGLAS

My father brought many voices to the people. The one
that will ring loudest to me, however, is his own. The way
he loved was the way I felt after his spirit flew into
my heart when he died. I was hungry to love and could
only hope to help as many people as he did. May his spirit
live on forever.

—DAVID GRAHAM
(son of rock promoter BILL GRAHAM)

My dad had a left eye that twinkled out of control when
he was happy. Making that happen was a key motivator
in my life until the day he died.

—JIM LEHRER *(PBS news anchor)*

Sometimes we would go for walks down the mile-long
east pier at the harbor. We would go on Friday evening
or sometimes on a Sunday night. Those were the times
we would talk. He would sometimes walk behind me
and then insert his thumbs between my shoulder blades
and say, "Stand up straight, lad, don't slouch, be proud."
It irritated me and I'd mumble something. He'd say,
"Don't mumble, no one ever understands what you're
saying, you know. Those bloody adenoids, you should have
elocution lessons."

"Diphthongs and monothongs," I mumbled.
"What's that?"
"Elocution."
"Really?"
"Yeah."

I liked him then, without his worries. He'd hide on
me. Simply disappear. I would be talking away and then
I would look beside me and he'd have gone. Usually he'd
just drop behind and then jump over the wall and walk
along parallel with me but out of sight. Other times
he'd simply sit on one of the green wooden benches
and hide behind his newspaper. I would be frightened, then
I'd feign indifference, then he'd pop up. . . . One day he
put his arms around my shoulders and we both stared
out to sea beyond the Kish lightship. We stood there
awhile and then he lifted his other arm and pointed into
the distance.

"Eastward ho," he said.

—BOB GELDOF

Since I've been playing organized football, I've paid tribute
to the king, my father, by wearing a shirt with his likeness
on it. It feels good wearing it, because he's right there
with me. It gives me the power every time. The one
time I didn't wear it, I broke my ankle.

—ROHAN MARLEY
(son of reggae singer BOB MARLEY,
who died from cancer in 1981)

That last night of Daddy's life was hell. He was sweating
bullets, flaying his arms, kicking his feet, looking like he
was fighting off the devil. [My brother] Leon went in
there—calm and centered—and, miraculously, comforted
him during his moment of maximum need.

I went in afterwards. He'd stopped struggling. I could
see the light in his eyes. He'd surrendered. It was scary,
but also beautiful. I kissed him on the lips.

"I love you," I said.

"Boy . . . ," he whispered, "I love you too."

He closed his eyes. He was gone.

—SMOKEY ROBINSON

I miss him very much. He was just fun, you know? He was always someone you really, really looked forward to seeing. He could be tough, but he was just such an adventure. If it wasn't a football game in the backyard, it was running a river in Colorado, or skiing, or going in a sailboat race, or learning how to water ski, or doing whatever the heck it might be. It was just an adventure.

I remember even when my father was thinking of running for president—and even after my grandfather was paralyzed and after my uncle had been killed and my grandfather couldn't talk—my father would go down and talk to him. And he wouldn't do anything of real importance without first having talked to my grandfather. And while nobody else could understand him, my father could understand. And that's what I miss. I just miss having somebody to figure it all out with. I just miss him for our family. I miss him. I miss him for me. I miss him for all of us. I miss him for my mom.

You know, it's just sad.

—JOE KENNEDY
(U.S. Representative
from Massachusetts,
son of ROBERT F. KENNEDY)

Permissions and Acknowledgments

Preface

Barbara Walters. From *The 50th Barbara Walters Special,* ABC Television, November 29, 1988.
Chet Atkins. From "I Still Can't Say Goodbye" by Chet Atkins. Copyright © 1987. By Chet Atkins.

1. Legacies

John Turturro. Author's interview.
Larry King. Author's interview.
Kinky Friedman. Author's interview.
Patrick Swayze. Reprinted courtesy of *People,* September 10, 1984. By permission.
Arlo Guthrie. Author's interview.
James Joyce. January 17, 1932, letter to Harriet Shaw Weaver, from *Selected Letters of James Joyce,* by James Joyce, edited by Richard Ellmann. Copyright © 1957, 1966, renewed 1985 by The Viking Press, Inc.; Copyright © 1966, 1975 by F. Lionel Munro as Administrator of the Estate of James Joyce. Used by permission of Viking Penguin, a division of Penguin Books USA, Inc.
Francis Ford Coppola. Reprinted with permission of Charles Scribner's Sons, an imprint of Macmillan Publishing Company from *Coppola: A Biography,* by Peter Cowie. Copyright © 1990 by Peter Cowie.
Fred Rogers. Author's interview.
Reggie Jackson. From *Reggie,* by Reggie Jackson and Mike Lupica. Copyright © 1984 by Reggie Jackson and Mike Lupica. Reprinted by permission of Villard Books, a division of Random House, Inc.

Ted Turner IV. Author's interview.

Allen Ginsberg. Author's interview.

Chuck Yeager. From *Yeager An Autobiography,* by General Chuck Yeager and Leo Janos. Copyright © 1985 by Yeager, Inc. Used by permission of Bantam Books, a division of Bantam Doubleday Dell Publishing Group, Inc.

Sam Shepard. From *Sam Shepard: The Life and Work of an American Dreamer* by Ellen Oumano. Copyright © 1986 by Ellen Oumano. St. Martin's Press.

Ed Eckstine. Author's interview.

Romano Mussolini. Reprinted courtesy of *Entertainment Weekly,* August 13, 1993, "Swingin' in the Reign" by Romano Mussolini. With permission.

Burt Reynolds. Reprinted with permission from *TV Guide* Magazine, April 25, 1992, "Burt Reynolds" by Mary Murphy. Copyright © 1992 by News America Publications, Inc. With permission.

Sean Lennon. From *Fathers* by Jon Winokur. Copyright © 1993 by Jon Winokur.

Bruce Springsteen. From *Bruce Springsteen: In His Own Words,* by John Duffy. Copyright © 1993 Omnibus Press. By Permission.

Robert F. Kennedy, Jr. Reprinted from *Newsday,* June 3, 1993, "The R.F.K Legacy" by Jack Sirica. And from "Sonya Live on CNN," June 3, 1993.

Wynton Marsalis. Author's interview.

2. Lessons

Bob Geldof. From *Is That It?* by Bob Geldof. Copyright © 1986 by Bob Geldof. Used with the permission of Grove/Atlantic Monthly Press.

Warren Beatty. From *Fathers* by Jon Winokur. Copyright © 1993 by Jon Winokur.

Rock Brynner. From *Yul: The Man Who Would be King,* by Rock Brynner. Copyright © 1990 by Simon & Schuster, Inc.

Jack Benny. From *Sunday Nights at Seven: The Jack Benny Story,* by Jack Benny and his daughter Joan. Copyright © 1990 by Joan Benny. Used by permission of Warner Books, Inc.

Michael Caine. From *What's It All About,* by Michael Caine. Copyright © 1992 by Stoke Films Ltd. Reprinted by permission of Random House, Inc.

Anthony Quinn. From *The Original Sin,* by Anthony Quinn. Copyright © 1972 by Anthony Quinn. By permission of Little, Brown and Company.

Ethan Browne. From *Interview,* June 1993.

Jackson Browne. From *Interview,* June 1993.

Jeff Kent. Author's interview.

Earvin "Magic" Johnson. From *My Life,* by Earvin Magic Johnson with William Novak. Copyright © 1992 Random House, Inc.

Frankie Faison. Author's interview.

Arlo Guthrie. Author's interview

Matthew Broderick. Reprinted from *Parade,* May 2, 1993. "In Step with Matthew Broderick" by James Brady.

Arthur Ashe, Jr. From *Advantage Ashe,* by Arthur Ashe, Jr. As told to Clifford George Gewecke, Jr. Copyright © Coward-McCann, Inc.

Arthur Marx. Reprinted from *Playboy,* January 1984.

Larry King. Author's interview.

Jimmy Scott. From the *Village Voice,* Winter 1988, *Voice Rock & Roll Quarterly,* "All the Way with Jimmy Scott" by Jimmy McDonough.

Mel Gibson. Reprinted courtesy of *Entertainment Weekly,* August 20, 1993. "To Mel and Back" by Allen Barra. With permission.

Ron Reagan. Reprinted from *Playboy,* "What Fathers Know Best," January 1984.

Red Barber. From *Rhubarb in the Catbird Seat,* by Red Barber and Robert Creamer. Copyright © 1968 Doubleday & Company, Inc.

Bill Cosby. From *The Cosby Wit: His Life and Humor,* by Bill Adler. Copyright © 1986. Carrol & Graf.

Timothy Leary. Author's interview.

Jon Secada. Author's interview.

Ted Turner IV. Author's interview.

Kirk Douglas. From *The Ragman's Son,* by Kirk Douglas. Copyright © 1988 Kirk Douglas. Simon & Schuster, Inc.

Gus Van Sant, Jr. From *Interview,* June 1993.

Donald Trump. From *The Art of the Deal,* by Donald Trump. Copyright © 1987. Random House. Reprinted by permission Random House, Inc.

Reggie Jackson. From *Reggie* by Reggie Jackson and Mike Lupica. By permission.

Tony Huston. Reprinted with permission of Charles Scribner's Sons, an imprint of Macmillan Publishing Company, from *The Hustons,* by Lawrence Grobel. Copyright © 1989 by Lawrence Grobel.

Lee Iacocca. From *Iacocca: An Autobiography,* by Lee Iacocca with William Novak. Copyright © 1984 by Lee Iacocca. Used by permission of Bantam Books, a division of Bantam Doubleday Dell Publishing Group, Inc.

Jean Renoir. From *Renoir, My Father,* by Jean Renoir; translated by Randolph and Dorothy Weaver. Copyright © 1958, 1962 by Jean Renoir. By permission of Little, Brown and Company.

Julian Lennon. Reprinted courtesy of *People,* January 7, 1985. By permission.

Bud Yorkin. Author's interview.

Roman Polanski. From *Roman,* by Roman Polanski. Copyright © 1984 by Roman Polanski. William Morrow and Company, Inc. By permission.

3. Missed Opportunities

Mike Rutherford. From "The Living Years" by Mike Rutherford. Copyright © 1988 Michael Rutherford Ltd./ R& BA Music Ltd. / Hit & Run Music Publishing Ltd. By permission.

Harry S Truman. From *Truman,* by David McCullough. Simon & Schuster, Inc., 1992. By permission.

Daniel Day-Lewis. Reprinted courtesy of *People,* February 22, 1988. By permission.

Marvin Gaye. From *Entertainment Weekly,* April 2, 1993.

Sir Laurence Olivier. From *Confessions of an Actor,* by Laurence Olivier. Copyright © 1982 by Wheelshare Ltd. Reprinted by permission of Simon & Schuster, Inc.

Ed Eckstine. Author's interview.

Frankie Faison. Author's interview.

Bill Moyers. Reprinted courtesy of *People,* March 15, 1993. By permission.

Andrei Sakharov. From *Memoirs* by Andrei Sakharov. Translated from the Russian by Richard Lourie. Copyright © 1990. By permission of Alfred A. Knopf.

Matthew Nelson. Reprinted courtesy of *People,* August 5, 1991. By permission.

Dennis Potter. From *Potter on Potter,* by Dennis Potter, edited by Graham Fuller. Copyright © 1993 Faber & Faber. Reprinted by permission of the author.

Randy Newman. Author's interview.

Larry King. Author's interview.

Arlo Guthrie. Author's interview.

Bud Yorkin. Author's interview.

Robert Meeropol. From *What Happened to Their Kids?* by Malcolm Forbes with Jeff Bloch. Copyright © 1990 by Malcolm Forbes. Published by Simon & Schuster, Inc. By permission.

Allen Ginsberg. Section 2 from "Don't Grow Old" from *Collected Poems 1947–1980 (Record #1)* by Allen Ginsberg. Copyright

4. Clashes

Malcolm Forbes with Jeff Bloch. Copyright © 1990 by Malcolm Forbes. Published by Simon & Schuster, Inc. By permission.

John S.D. Eisenhower. From *Strictly Personal,* by John S.D. Eisenhower. Copyright © 1974 by John S.D. Eisenhower. Used by permission of Doubleday, a division of Bantam Doubleday Dell Publishing Group, Inc.

Philip Roth. From *Patrimony,* by Philip Roth. Copyright © 1990 by Philip Roth. Reprinted by permission of Simon & Schuster, Inc.

Hume Cronyn. From *A Terrible Liar,* by Hume Cronyn. Copyright © 1991 by Hume Cronyn. William Morrow and Company, Inc. By permission.

D. H. Lawrence. From *The Selected Letters of D. H. Lawrence,* edited by Diana Trilling. Farrar, Straus and Cudahy, Inc.

Pat Conroy. Reprinted from *Newsday,* November 4, 1991. "The Art of Hating—And Loving" by Kathryn McCormick.

Tobias Wolff. From *This Boy's Life,* by Tobias Wolff. Copyright © 1989 by Tobias Wolff. Used with the permission of Grove/Atlantic Monthly Press.

James Toney. Reprinted from *Sports Illustrated.*

Thomas J. Watson, Jr. From *Father, Son & Co.,* by Thomas J. Watson, Jr. Copyright © 1990 by Thomas J. Watson, Jr. Used by permission of Bantam Books, a division of Bantam Doubleday Dell Publishing Group, Inc.

William R. Hearst, Jr. The Associated Press.

David Nelson. From *Esquire,* "The Happy Happy Happy Nelsons," June 1971.

Bruce Springsteen. From *Bruce Springsteen: In His Own Words*, by John Duffy. By permission.

Dennis Miller. From *Fathers,* by Jon Winokur. Copyright © 1993 by Jon Winokur.

Spike Lee. From *What Black People Should Do Now,* by Ralph Wiley. Copyright © 1993. Alfred A. Knopf, Inc. By permission.

Little Richard. From *The Life and Times of Little Richard,* by Charles White. Copyright © 1984. Pocket Books.

Marvin Gaye. From *Divided Soul: The Life of Marvin Gaye,* by David Ritz. Copyright © 1985. McGraw-Hill. Reprinted by permission.

5. Silences

Bruce Springsteen. From *Bruce Springsteen: In His Own Words,* by John Duffy. By permission.

Peter Fonda. Reprinted from *Playboy,* January 1984.

Joe McGinniss. From *Heroes,* by Joe McGinniss. Copyright © 1976 by Joe McGinniss. Reprinted by permission of Sterling Lord Literistic, Inc.

Dr. Benjamin Spock. From *Spock on Spock,* by Mary Morgan. Copyright © 1989 by Benjamin M. Spock and Mary Morgan. Reprinted by permission of Pantheon Books, a division of Random House, Inc.

Hans Albert Einstein. From *What Happened to Their Kids?* by Malcolm Forbes with Jeff Bloch. Copyright © 1990 by Malcolm Forbes. Published by Simon & Schuster, Inc.

Kareem Abdul-Jabbar. From *Giant Steps* by Kareem Abdul-Jabbar. Copyright © 1983 by Kareem Abdul-Jabbar. Used by permission of Bantam Books, a division of Bantam Doubleday Dell Publishing Group, Inc.

Mark Harmon. Reprinted courtesy of *People.* By permission.

Michael Reagan. Reprinted from *Playboy,* January 1984.

Kirk Douglas. From *The Ragman's Son,* by Kirk Douglas, Copyright © 1988 by Kirk Douglas. Simon & Schuster, Inc. By permission Kirk Douglas.

Thurman Munson. From *Thurman Munson: An Autobiography,* by Thurman Munson with Martin Appel. Copyright © 1978 Tempo Books.

Richard Russo. Author's interview.

6. Absence

Charles Barkley. From *Outrageous,* by Charles Barkley & Roy S. Johnson. Copyright © 1992 by Charles Barkley & Roy S. Johnson. Reprinted by permission of Simon & Schuster, Inc.

Bo Jackson. From *Bo Knows Bo: The Autobiography of a Ballplayer,* by Bo Jackson and Dick Schaap. Copyright © 1990 by Bo Jackson and Dick Schaap. Used by permission of Doubleday, a division of Bantam Doubleday Dell Publishing Group, Inc.

Russell Baker. From *The Good Times,* by Russell Baker. Copyright © 1989 by Russell Baker. By permission William Morrow and Company, Inc.

Tom Cruise. Reprinted courtesy of *Entertainment Weekly,* December 11, 1992. By permission.

David Geffen. Reprinted courtesy of the *New York Times Magazine.* May 2, 1993. "David Geffen, Still Hungry," by Bernard Weinraub. By permission.

Sonny Bono. From *And the Beat Goes On,* by Sonny Bono. Copyright

7. What Happened to His Dreams?

8. What Did He Really Think?

Picking. Copyright © 1988 by Phil Niekro, Joe Niekro and Ken Picking. Contemporary Books.

Eugene O'Neill. From *O'Neill: Son & Artist,* by Louis Sheaffer. Copyright © 1973 by Louis Sheaffer. Little, Brown and Company. By permission.

Roger Baldwin. From *Roger Baldwin: Founder of the American Civil Liberties Union,* by Peggy Lamson. Copyright © 1976 by Peggy Lamson. Reprinted by permission of Houghton Mifflin Company. All rights reserved.

John S.D. Eisenhower. From *Strictly Personal,* by John S.D. Eisenhower. Copyright © 1974 by John S.D. Eisenhower. By permission.

Ed Eckstine. Author's interview.

John Updike. From "Son" from *Problems and Other Stories,* by John Updike. Copyright © 1973 by John Updike. Alfred A. Knopf, Inc. By permission.

Raymond Carver. "Photograph of My Father in His Twenty-Second Year" from *Fires: Essays, Poems & Stories.* Copyright © 1983 by Raymond Carver. Reprinted by permission of Capra Press, Santa Barbara.

Paul Auster. From *The Invention of Solitude,* by Paul Auster. Copyright © 1982 by Paul Auster. Used by permission of the Carol Mann Agency.

9. Things I'm Glad I Said to My Father

Benjamin Cheever. From *The Journals of John Cheever,* Introduction by Benjamin Cheever. Copyright © 1990 by Mary Cheever, Susan Cheever, Benjamin Cheever, and Federico Cheever. By permission of Alfred A. Knopf, Inc.

Paul Shaffer. Interview with Steven Dougherty. By permission.

Randy Newman. Author's interview

Smokey Robinson. From *Inside My Life,* by Smokey Robinson with David Ritz. Copyright © 1989 by Smokey Robinson and David Ritz. McGraw-Hill. By permission.

Donald Trump. From *Lost Tycoon: The Many Lives of Donald Trump,* by Harry Hurt III. Copyright © 1993. W.W. Norton.

Jeff Bridges. Reprinted from *Parade,* July 11, 1993. "What I Learned From Love" by Tom Seligson.

Jon Secada. Author's interview.

Michael Norman, Reprinted from the *New York Times Magazine,* June 15, 1980. Used by permission of Michael Norman.

10. Enduring Love

Randy Newman. Author's interview.

James Reston. From *Deadline,* by James Reston Copyright © 1991 by James Reston. Reprinted by permission of Random House, Inc.

Carl Lewis. From *Inside Track,* by Carl Lewis with Jeffrey Marx. Copyright © 1990 by Carl Lewis and Jeffrey Marx. Reprinted by permission of Simon & Schuster, Inc.

Theodore Roosevelt. From *Theodore Roosevelt: A Life,* by Nathan Miller. William Morrow and Company, Inc.

Loudon Wainwright III. "Sometimes I Forget," by Loudon Wainwright III. Copyright © 1992 Snowden Music, Inc. Used by permission.

Loudon Wainwright, Jr. From *Life,* June 1988. "The View from Here: Father's Day," by Loudon Wainwright, Jr.

Arlo Guthrie. Author's interview.

James Cagney. From *Cagney by Cagney,* by James Cagney. Copyright © 1976 by Doubleday, a division of Bantam Doubleday Dell Publishing Group, Inc. Used by permission of Doubleday, a division of Bantam Doubleday Dell Publishing Group, Inc.

Sergei Khrushchev. From *Khrushchev on Khrushchev,* by Sergei Khrushchev. Used by permission of Little, Brown and Company.

Louie Anderson. From *Dear Dad,* by Louie Anderson. Copyright © 1989 by Louzelle Productions, Inc. Used by permission of Viking Penguin, a division of Penguin Books USA Inc.

Osgood Perkins. From *Interview,* June 1993.

Hume Cronyn. From *A Terrible Liar,* by Hume Cronyn. By permission.

Tyrone Bogues. From the *New York Times,* August 15, 1993. "How a Father May Figure into an Athlete's Life," by William C. Rhoden.

Sam Keen. From *Fire in the Belly: On Being a Man,* by Sam Keen. Copyright © 1991 by Sam Keen. Bantam Books.

Mario Cuomo. From *Diaries of Mario M. Cuomo: The Campaign for Governor,* by Mario M. Cuomo. Copyright © 1984 by Random House, Inc. Used by permission.

Ron Karnaugh. Reprinted from *People,* September 14, 1992; the *New York Times,* August 1, 1992; and United Press International, August 5, 1992.

Anthony Quinn. From *The Original Sin,* by Anthony Quinn. By permission.

Kirk Douglas. From *The Ragman's Son,* by Kirk Douglas, Copyright © 1988 by Kirk Douglas. Simon & Schuster, Inc.

David Graham. From *Bill Graham Presents,* by Bill Graham and Robert Greenfield. Copyright © 1992 by The Estate of Bill Graham. Used by permission of Doubleday, a division of Bantam Doubleday Dell Publishing Group, Inc.

Jim Lehrer, from *A Bus of My Own,* by Jim Lehrer. Copyright © 1992 by Penguin, USA.

Bob Geldof. From *Is That It?* by Bob Geldof. By permission.

Rohan Marley. From *Interview,* June 1993.

Smokey Robinson. From *Inside My Life,* by Smokey Robinson with David Ritz. Copyright © 1989 by Smokey Robinson and David Ritz. McGraw-Hill. By permission.

Joe Kennedy. From the *Washington Post Sunday Magazine,* June 6, 1993. "Settling In" by Walt Harrington.

Index

Abdul-Jabbar, Kareem, 67–68
Ali, Muhammad, 51
Anderson, Louie, 105–107
Ashe, Arthur, Jr., 24
Auster, Paul, 91–92

Baker, Russell, 74
Baldwin, Roger, 88–89
Barber, Red, 26–27
Barkley, Charles, 72–73
Beatty, Warren, 15
Benny, Jack, 16–17
Bernstein, Carl, 83–84
Bogues, Tyrone, 108
Bono, Sonny, 75–77
Bridges, Jeff, 97
Broderick, Matthew, 24
Browne, Ethan (son of Jackson
   Browne), 19
Browne, Jackson, 19
Broyard, Anatole, 70
Brynner, Rock (son of Yul
   Brynner), 15–16, 55

Cagney, James, 104–105
Caine, Michael, 17
Capra, Frank, 48
Carver, Raymond, 90–91
Cheever, Benjamin (son of John
   Cheever), 95
Churchill, Randolph (son of
   Winston Churchill), 56
Claiborne, Craig, 87
Conroy, Pat, 59
Coppola, Francis Ford, 6

Cosby, Bill, 27
Cronyn, Hume, 57–58, 107–108
Cruise, Tom, 75
Cuomo, Mario, 109

Day-Lewis, Daniel, 39–40
Douglas, Kirk, 29, 69–70,
   110–111

Eckstine, Ed (son of Billy
   Eckstine), 10–11, 40–41,
   89–90
Einstein, Hans Albert (son of
   Albert Einstein), 67
Eisenhower, John S.D. (son of
   Dwight D. Eisenhower), 56, 89

Faison, Frankie, 22–23, 41–42
Fonda, Peter, 65
Ford, Jack, 78
Friedman, Kinky, 4

Gaye, Marvin, 40, 63–64
Geffen, David, 75
Geldof, Sir Bob, 15, 111–112
Gibson, Mel, 26
Ginsberg, Allen, 9, 46–47
Gleason, Jackie, 78
Graham, David (son of Bill
   Graham), 111
Guthrie, Arlo, 5–6, 23–24, 46,
   52, 86, 103–104